THE 60%
SOLUTION
Rethinking
Healthcare

THE 60%
SOLUTION
Rethinking
Healthcare

TODD FURNISS

Clovercroft Publishing

The 60% Solution: Rethinking Healthcare

Published by Clovercroft Publishing, Franklin, Tennessee

Edited by Nancy Hancock

Cover and Interior Design by Adept Content Solutions

Printed in the United States of America

ISBN   978-1-954437-03-6
eISBN 978-1-954437-05-0

CONTENTS

Introduction
THE STORY BEGINS
WITH A CRASH

In 1977, Atlanta, Georgia, was beginning a growth cycle that has continued to this day. Like many urban areas, Atlanta's downtown was in the early stages of becoming more vibrant. Grand hotels, like the Hyatt Regency, with innovative architecture designed by John Portman featured prominently in the remaking of the city. The city's light rail system was being developed, there was an emerging music scene, and businesses like UPS, Coca Cola, and Delta Airlines were a part of the growing business landscape. Atlanta also had, and still has, one of the busiest airports in the world, which was then known as Atlanta Municipal Airport.

On April 4, 1977, my parents were traveling home to Virginia Beach from Huntsville, Alabama, and flying into Atlanta to make a connecting flight. My father was a trial lawyer who did a great deal of work for insurance companies. They called it "insurance defense." He was on the opposite side of the "ambulance chasers," a category of lawyer my father and mother held in dim regard. My mother was "studying the law" under my father, a way to sidestep law school and still qualify to sit for the bar exam. She straddled the roles of law student and paralegal, helping my father and his partners in preparing and trying cases.

My parents had flown to Huntsville to take depositions for a case they were working on. Depositions can be long, grueling affairs and often require preparation in advance and great focus during the deposition. It is not uncommon for counsel to leave exhausted. After completing their work, my parents made their way to the airport. My father's tie would have been loosened, signaling the end of work for the day, and he would probably have had a beer or two while waiting to board the plane. My mother was dressed professionally in a skirt, a blouse, and a jacket. She was also wearing leather boots, which would prove to be both important and unfortunate.

We know now that the pilots were not given a complete story about the threatening weather. Not only did the FAA not give them the whole story, neither did the airline. As with many life tragedies, a collection of mishaps proved to be contributors: computer systems failure was only one part of the problem, routing was a problem, and jet engine design was a problem. Years later, my mother would tell me that she and her fellow passengers were told that they might experience some turbulence along the way to Atlanta, nothing more. Later, my reading of excerpts of NTSB reports would confirm that the pilots had not been not told of the weather risk that lay before them and thus could not have informed the passengers. This failure to communicate was not because the computer and radar systems in the control towers malfunctioned, but rather the humans responsible for communicating vital weather information to the flight crew failed to do their job.

A squall of heavy thunderstorms had formed a wall directly across Southern Airways Flight 242's fifty-five-minute flight path as the plane approached Atlanta. These storms dumped tremendous volumes of water onto the plane in the form of rain and hail, and the plane was hit by lightning. The engines were not designed to ingest and could not process the torrent of water the rainstorms produced. The left engine was mechanically drowning, and it was the first to go. Then, the autopilot went out. The pilots flew the plane by hand the best they could, but thirteen seconds later the right engine went out. They were down to 13,000 feet with no power from either engine as the storm raged around them.

Airplanes are big metal rocks that fall quickly without power to move them forward through the air. Southern Airways Flight 242 was no different, and the age of the plane may have made it worse. The plane was dropping in the sky, and soon the flight was slowiy progressing forward at only 4,600 feet.

The air traffic controllers monitoring the flight tried to guide them to nearby Dobbins Air Force base, which was seventeen miles away and had the requisite length of runway. More importantly, in case something went wrong, Dobbins had emergency responders and equipment to minimize damage and injury. However, at only 4,600 feet with an airspeed of 126 knots, the plane was not going to make Dobbins. The plane simply did not have the engine capability, air speed or altitude to get there without power.

The flight attendants did an impressive job of trying to calm the passengers as the flight became increasingly violent. All passengers were told to take off their shoes, or their boots in my mother's case, so that they could safely make it down the emergency slides should they need to use them to exit the plane once landed. Passengers were instructed to get in the tuck position to brace for impact with the ground.

Once the engines stopped, their silence was overwhelmed by the roar of the rain and hail pummeling the fuselage of the aircraft as it quickly descended. They were not only descending; they were also slowing down. Nine minutes after the first engine failed, the pilots spotted a highway and instantly decided to try to land the plane on it. "Uh, we're putting it on the highway; we're down to nothing," were the pilot's recorded words. The next one minute and thirty-three seconds of the final flight recording were exchanges of courage, encouragement, and support. The ninety-fourth second was the sound of the crash that took the lives of both pilots, sixty-three passengers, and nine people on the ground. Only twenty passengers and two crew members survived the crash, though fewer would survive more than twelve months due to the severity of the injuries they sustained during the crash.

The heroic landing was executed by experienced pilots doing the best they could with brutally flawed equipment supported by error-prone bureaucrats. They had no engines. They had limited electronics. They had bad information. Still, the outcome might have been far different had the pilots been able to stop the aircraft once it was on the ground. Tragically, the plane hit a gas station just after touching down, which triggered an abrupt and fiery explosion. My mother later told me that she and my father were both calm and confident until the moment the crash occurred. The flight attendants were reassuring, and the announcements from the cockpit were reassuring. The real horror did not commence in earnest until the landing.

I can now say that it may have been a blessing that my father was killed instantly. He did not have to go through everything my mother endured. He was spared the horror and pain that began the moment that explosion occurred. The standard emergency landing instructions my mother followed proved unimaginably bad.

As was the style of the day, my mother was wearing panty-hose under her skirt and boots. What many did not know at the time was that the boots would have protected her legs and feet. Instead, with no boots to shield her legs from the heat of the fires, her pantyhose melted into her skin. Despite horrific pain, she dragged herself through the wreckage of the aircraft in search of her husband only to find him dead. Then the pain of her burns and other injuries overtook her, and she passed out. She was taken to Grady Memorial Hospital. She lost three toes to amputation. She also suffered a fractured skull, broken vertebrae, and catastrophic multiple injuries. Two thirds of her body was covered with third-degree burns. Her unseen injuries would prove to be just as bad, if not worse, than those that were visible.

In addition to being close to the site of the crash, Grady Memorial Hospital had the benefit of being an enormous and highly regarded medical facility that was known as the best burn unit east of the Mississippi. The staff at Grady were endearingly polite. The men were gentlemen, and it was not uncommon to see the male doctors in bow ties, khaki pants, and cordovan penny loafers. "Yes, ma'am" and "yes, sir" were frequent and customary responses.

To the best of my knowledge, all the crash victims of Southern Airways Flight 242 who were not taken directly to the morgue were taken to Grady, which was a giant complex system anchored by a county hospital. Its mission to provide compassionate, high-quality healthcare my mother needed. Grady would be my mother's home for a very long time.

My grandmother's arrival at our home in Virginia Beach was the first cue that something was wrong—she never came to the house uninvited. We loved her dearly and respected her immensely. Mimi had been a single mother from the time my grandfather died in his second plane crash during the Korean War. She was independent, sweet, and tough. Even at seventeen years old and a few weeks from graduating from high school, I knew something was wrong when I saw her stride purposefully up the brick walk to our front door. My fourteen-year-old brother, fifteen-year-old sister, and I were playing in the yard, and I entered the house through the kitchen to greet her there. It was Monday, April 4, 1977, at about 6:30 p.m.

Mimi solemnly told me that the plane carrying my parents had crashed, but she did not have any information beyond that confirmation. My brother, Eddie, and my sister, Berkeley, came in and were told the news. We all huddled in the TV room to watch the breaking story—this was 1977, long before the web, social media, cable TV, or CNN. We waited anxiously until the eleven o'clock ABC news broadcast, which did not say much, only that the plane had crashed and there were many fatalities. The crash of Southern 242 was (and remains) the worst aviation accident in Georgia's history.

We take constant and varied communication tools for granted today, but then we relied on telephone land lines. Even though our modern, push button phone was an upgrade from the rotary dial, we had no alternative but to wait by the phone for calls we dreaded.

Fortunately, we had a telephone in the same room where the television was located because we were glued to both, hoping desperately for any whiff of information. In our first telephone call, we were told that my mother had died but my father had lived. In a second call, we were told that both of our parents had died. Finally, we learned that dad had died and mom had lived. The networks signed off shortly after the eleven o'clock news leaving us in a state of shock. The silence was deafening and none of us could move.

Uncertain about what would happen next or what to do, the three of us, after a sleepless night, decided to go to school. We believed that was what our parents would want, and Mimi agreed. Ours was a family of clear expectations and strong rules. Besides, while we were eager to get to my mother's bedside, we had no family or friends in Atlanta. I don't even recall if we had a credit card to have paid for the plane ticket or a hotel. As our parents planned to return the same day, we had been left with a stocked refrigerator and given some cash to buy what we needed until our parents returned from their trip.

Mimi would take the first flight available to Atlanta on April 5, 1977. She could be more agile by herself, and free to check on Mom's full situation and assess her status and needs while advocating for her in a complex system. Even if we'd wanted to see Mom, a hospital spokesperson told us we would not be able to due to the extent of her injuries. She would undergo dozens of operations over the coming days and was in a heavily medicated state. We would take flights that weekend.

The days between the crash and our flight to Atlanta were filled with well-wishers. Throngs of friends and family members visited the house nightly bringing food, concern, worry, sorrow, and sharing some uplifting memories. Mr. Yee, one of my father's best friends, owned a Chinese restaurant and came by daily with huge trays of food. The crush of goodwill remains to this day appreciated, but it was overwhelming at the time.

Going to see my mother in Grady Memorial Hospital was a physical, logistical, emotional, and financial ordeal. In retrospect, I never appreciated the extent to which it was challenging on each and every one of those dimensions.

We would start planning the trip by coordinating with my grandmother as to the "right time" to come. My mother was fiercely proud and had clear views on virtually every topic. Like many mothers, she was demanding. At the same time, she did not want to be a burden, least of all to her children. Family was important. School was important. Achievement was important. I had to balance my mother's willingness and unwillingness to see me and my siblings and other family members with school and our ability to get there. In 1977, the approximately 700-mile journey was about fifteen hours by car and a couple of hours by plane. While the airline would pay for us to fly to Atlanta, that option didn't fulfill our needs. We decided that I would drive. In addition to having better control of departure and return, we would also have our own car while in Atlanta.

Once we arrived in Atlanta, we were housed at the Grand Hyatt, where my grandmother was already staying, all of us, at the expense of the airline responsible for the crash. The Hyatt was only about a mile from the hospital, so it was convenient. We would meet my grandmother at the hotel and plan the visit to Grady Memorial, typically for the next day.

Once we arrived at the hospital and before we were allowed into Mom's room, we had to "scrub in" with Betadine, put on booties, masks, hair bonnets, and the gowns used at that time. Only then could we enter the room with the 360-degree bed where, when I first saw her, my mother was positioned lying on her stomach.

My mother's legs were where they were supposed to be, but they were unrecognizable. Seared by the fire and her melted pantyhose, her legs were bloody open wounds. Strips of flesh had been taken out of her back and grafted into more severely burned areas on her legs and feet. Her bottom was the only part of her body that was covered with a thin piece of paper, because anything with more weight would have been agonizingly painful for her in ways that I could not imagine. Berkeley and Mimi always seemed so much stronger than I felt. For me, my stomach and every adjacent organ felt as though they were being gripped and twisted until the surrealism of the burn unit set in and it seemed so horrible and antiseptic as to not to be real. As much as we hated seeing her like this, our mother hated us seeing her like this more.

Our visits to Atlanta continued, and we would meet my grandmother and plan each hospital visit. I was told that over the approximately five months she was hospitalized there, Mom had over 100 major operations. Roughly five months after arriving at Grady Memorial Hospital, my mother was released to the rehab center at Emory University to begin the grueling process of physical rehabilitation. Emory, also located in Atlanta, was not far away. Rehabilitation took almost three months, but fortunately that expense paid was also paid for under the feeble settlement into which my mother was forced. Mimi was posted in Atlanta almost entirely until she and Mom returned home nearly eight months after the accident.

My sister, brother, and I clung to some semblance of normalcy when at home in Virginia Beach. Mom's brother, Jim, was very helpful and would check on us frequently. Her older sister stayed for a little while too, but we were very independent and we had a routine of our own running the house, finishing school, and in my case getting geared up for college in the fall.

I took over bill paying responsibilities, often helped by Jim or my younger sister, Berkeley. We were always eager to hear good news on Mom's progress and we missed her terribly. We could not think of any outcome where she would not come home. All the while, we were grieving our father's death.

Every aspect of my mother's life was forever changed by the injuries she sustained in that crash. The doctors performed miracle after miracle in repairing everything from broken bones to torn ligaments to destroyed toes to burned flesh. Her treatment and recovery would be an ultra-long endurance test of indescribable pain and rehabilitation before she could walk in any form. She would never again be able to walk easily, so she was always on the hunt for "comfortable" shoes, "attractive" foldable canes, or "useful" crutches. She could not ascend stairs, so we needed a device to help her get up and down the staircase in our home. As an aside, it is not without irony that her father had survived one plane crash and died in a second plane crash, her husband died in a plane crash, her son (my brother, Eddie) later died in a plane crash while the other men in her family served without injury in World War I, World War II, the Korean War, and Vietnam. In many ways, my mother had been as severely injured as someone who barely survived military conflict. Oddly, neither my brother, sister, grandmother, nor I ever had a fear of flying.

In October of 1977, my mother was able to leave Atlanta and return to Virginia Beach, though not to our home in Virginia Beach. She had to stay in a first-floor hotel room fit for those with disabilities, which thankfully was close to our family home where Berkeley, Eddie, and I remained. Eddie and Berkeley were still in high school. Both were bright, independent, and good students. I got a tennis scholarship at Old Dominion, only a thirty-minute drive from home where I lived through most of college.

My mother's initial hotel stay in Virginia Beach was to accommodate her while our family home was renovated to meet her needs. Work on the renovations could not be completed until we knew what her needs were, and we could not know what her needs would be until we understood the outcome of the rehabilitation. Then, there was the issue of negotiating with the airline and their insurer to pay for all of it.

The Importance of Spirit and Will When Faced with the Challenge of Transition

The final settlement with the airline had a few components and numbers that were too small. The payments covered all of the work done at Grady and Emory, our family's travel expenses to Atlanta for my siblings, my grandmother, and me and the costs for the renovations to our house so that my mother could live there. All of this had occurred at a point in our nation's history that long preceded the Americans with Disabilities Act, but which would give us much more empathy for it. The settlement also included a lump-sum payment for my mother which was very modest, and an annuity that would last for the remainder of her life but was not adjusted over time for inflation. Critically important though, the settlement did not cover the costs of health insurance for my mother after she left Emory's rehab unit.

While Mom lost so much of her quality of life immediately and continued to lose more over time, she never lost her charm. Everyone who met her was charmed by my mother. It would be more than a year later that she would start dating, and it would be almost four years later that she would marry a fantastic public finance lawyer named Howard Whitaker, Jr., or "Whit" as we called him.

Initially, Whit would split his time between New York City and Virginia Beach. Mom would soon travel to New York City, ironically by plane. She would always check in with the pilots as she boarded each flight and check the weather, but she would never fear flying. Later in her life, she would work on flight safety issues with Congress and the NTSB.

Whit went on to lead the opening of the San Francisco office of his large New York law firm, then move to Miami, and ultimately take a job as senior bond counsel with Dade County. Whit's career moves were always made with due consideration of my mother's health and, importantly, her access to health insurance. He was very fond of the Dade County finance group, but he refused to be forced to retire at any age, which meant that he would have insurance for himself and my mother through a combination of Medicare and coverage provided through the firm until he lost his battle with cancer in August of 2004.

My mother endured acute ebbs and flows with her health with a slow but steady downward trend line while married to Whit and for the seven years that she lived after Whit died, but her charm could be mustered even in her darkest hours and produce the outcomes she desired. Dedicated and very compassionate to the causes she championed, her doctors wanted to do everything they could to make her as comfortable as possible. So, too, did the pharmacists. Exceptionally smart and armed with a keen sense of human nature, my mother learned how to manage bureaucrats, caregivers, and the healthcare system very effectively. Her pain was intolerable and incessant, and it ultimately led to addictions and the consequential behavioral and psychological issues.

My mother's medical issues led to financial issues not only immediately following the accident but for the next thirty-five years. The crash settlement included what would now be considered a very modest cash settlement for my mother and for each of the minor children. What was not covered by insurance had to be paid for by our family, including Whit after he and Mom married, and those expenses were daunting. Clothing costs were driven by what Mom could comfortably wear, with shoes being a particular problem. Canes, walkers, crutches, eyeglasses, chairs, mattresses, bed linens, over-the-counter medicines, prescription medicines, bandages, gauze, tape . . . the list went on and on. Fortunately, we could muster the resources to pay for these expenses. Others would have been overwhelmed by them.

When Whit was diagnosed with cancer in 2001, my mother's needs increased to include nurses at home. Whit, too, would have nurses at home until he passed in 2004. After Whit died, we moved Mom to an assisted care facility, returning her to her hometown of Virginia Beach. Having reached the age of sixty-five, she was in the right demographic, but her needs were well beyond that of other sixty-five-year-old residents, and soon, the facility concluded that assisted living was also not possible.

My mother's care required daily attention to help her with everything from dressing to eating to managing medicines. She could not drive. Getting into a car went from uncomfortable and awkward to acutely painful to not worth it. Her inability to get in a vehicle led to decreasing mobility and decreasing socializing. She lost touch with her friends. She had trouble getting to doctor's appointments. The doctors at her living facility were incapable of helping her or even of understanding her medical condition.

Care facilities that initially promised that my mother could "age in place," meaning that she could move from one area of the facility to another as her changing needs for care demanded, were either just trying to fill beds or not being truthful with us. Instead, the promised transitions from one area to another would be delayed or denied, so she had to move from one facility to another. This uncertainty and seemingly endless series of relocations led to sadness, depression, and a sense of being a "burden" to the family.

Memory care living was possible only because we augmented my mother's care with round-the-clock nursing care, which was privately funded by my family and me to the tune of over $15,000 per month in addition to the cost of the medical care, the medications, and the memory care facility itself.

Our mother's life continued as an endless series of ups and downs. She typically averaged one operation and two bouts of pneumonia leading to three hospitalizations each year after the accident. In between those hospitalizations, she might also throw five cocktail parties to connect people to one another, chair a fundraiser for one of the charities she supported, and work with Congress on flight safety issues.

A Focus on Care

The injuries, surgeries, and illnesses accumulated, and Mom's health deteriorated. Her life became more and more narrowly focused on getting through each day, and the bounce of days when she felt good and capable slowly flatlined to a numbing focus on getting through another day. Her spirit and relentless optimism seemed to draw upon a bottomless reservoir of human will. She would regularly say, often when confronted with inexorable pain or a dispiriting prognosis, "this too shall pass."

Moving from Georgia, where the accident occurred, to Virginia, where she would live until she married Whit, to New York, to live with Whit, to California, where Whit would transfer, to Florida, where Whit would work, and again back to Virginia meant that she could not get help from the doctors whom she had educated and to whom she had become accustomed—state licensing laws made and continue to make practicing medicine across state lines illegal. But consider what had to happen at each point of geographical and medical transition: the doctors, nurses, therapists, and technicians at Emory and every location subsequent to Emory had no initial knowledge of my mother's medical history or current status nor the countless and horrific injuries my mother had sustained.

Worse yet, the problems and the pain were so unimaginable that they could not be trusted. Doctors, nurses and non-medical personnel oftentimes would simply not believe my mother when she told them of the problems she was experiencing or why, thus adding genuine insult to genuine injury.

Each move required the physical copying and transfer of what became a large roomful of medical records stacked floor to ceiling and wall to wall. Those records, even today, would have to be "faxed," to each new healthcare provider, printed, filed, and stored—an obviously untenable solution. There was no portable electronic health record that could be used. The recipient caregivers would have to ingest, synthesize, and be able to diagnose based on their understanding of the issue before them in light of the documented medical history. In each new city and with each hospitalization, all caregivers had to be quickly educated on my mother's needs and develop appropriate recommendations for her care, but they would not be paid for this work. Simple things like telephone calls and video calls that could leverage experience and very specific knowledge of the problems my mother had could not be leveraged, nor could the "continuity of care" observations of those physicians my mother had seen for years be leveraged to expedite care needs.

A Bridge to the Future—Why This Story Matters

I don't pretend that the propositions in this book will solve the problems my siblings and I experienced while caring for my mother. Instead, I want to use those experiences to highlight the additional dimensions of care that my mother required because of her complicated, long medical history following the crash. Those dimensions include understanding what was required, how much was charged, who was obligated to pay, who paid, keeping records of the services that have been performed, and the administration associated with all of it—record keeping, filing, submitting, following up, dealing with claim rejection, dealing with pharmacy issues, and needing medications that insurance won't allow or won't pay for—are sadly troubling in their negative synergy. In other words, the collection of administrative activities is both complex and creates complexity; not only does one medical interaction affect the other and create additional work, but as a result is that the industry exacts additional emotional and financial tolls from everyone involved.

The policy solutions offered to date produce rules, governmental regulations, commercial regulations, and operational outcomes that are inefficient, suboptimal, and emotionally and financially expensive. Further, the majority of recommended changes are anchored in an ideology and are designed to serve its interests. But the many issues my family faced and that healthcare consumers, insurance companies, caregivers, and other stakeholders face show very clearly that a solution driven by ideological purity would never work. Single payor, by itself, won't work. Pure consumerism with no insurance won't work. Insurance, by itself, is not insurance and won't work. *The 60% Solution* addresses the issues each of these solutions overlooks and puts forward a solution to each of them that realistically addresses the challenges each one poses.

This book proposes a solution that builds on what we have learned as an industry, as a nation, and it has been inspired by the author's experiences. I believe and hope that everyone can benefit from this tour. We will revisit my mother's example where we can see the full dimension of the healthcare needs of the US population though the lens of my mother's tragic experience :

She was involved in accident: catastrophic insurance.

She would then have pre-existing conditions through no fault of her own: no rejection for pre-existing conditions.

She had a need for personalized care: primary care physicians.

She had a need for someone to learn her problems quickly: medical records and their portability.

She needed a way to pay for physician visits, medical supplies, and deductibles: health savings accounts.

She would struggle with neurological and behavioral problems: mental health.

She had the issue of someone else with whom her economic and health interest were not aligned paying the bills.

Issue Identification and Illumination

In the beginning of this discussion of my mother's changing needs for healthcare support of every kind, I mentioned that there were housing, financial, and legal issues in addition to the medical issues, all intertwined.

First, let's look at what happens when someone else is paying for your healthcare. This is a financial issue, but legal issues arise out of it also.

My mother was in an accident that was clearly not her fault and clearly was the fault of the airline. In legal terms, that is a "tort," and it links the person responsible for the injury with financial responsibility to pay for damages arising out of that injury. The airline's economic interest was to relieve themselves of liability as quickly and subject to as little expense as possible. After all, they were trying to run an airline for profit. Any amounts paid to victims of a crash reduced their earnings. It was a zero-sum game. The result was that Southern Airways paid for the care my mother received while in Grady and during her rehabilitations at Emory and that was it. They did not pay, directly or indirectly, for her to receive any care at any time after that despite the fact that her injuries would not only never heal but would actually cause cascading problems in almost every facet of her life for the rest of her life.

Insurance companies have their own complex system of economic incentives. If they can save money by paying as little as possible, they will. If they push the limits, which they may, they can do so while not violating the terms of the insurance policy under which a patient receives care, and they most certainly will. Oddly, they don't care much about the prices of care going up, but they do mind the amount they pay out, or their "loss ratio," going up. Their indifference as to the former is because no one pays "list price." As to the latter, and it is particularly the case with publicly traded insurance companies, they want to maximize near-term earnings, which they do by putting a tight clamp on outgoing payments. Whether by delaying payment by contesting the code on the claim, the amount of the claim, or some other matter, they are going to do what they can to hold on to their cash for as long as possible. Remember that the insured is paying the insurance company *in advance for something that is statistically unlikely to happen!* (We will discuss this later in the book when we discuss how insurance premium are determined and paid.)

The Legal Context of Healthcare

Long ago, I was in my first year of law school muddling through the mandatory coursework that included "Contracts." We learned about a concept the gravity of which continues to unfold for me to this day. It was "privity of contract." This simple term has enormous implications for everyone every day but has particularly pointed impact when it comes to dealing with healthcare issues.

Privity of contract addresses the relationship, rights, and obligations between the parties to a contract. Recall Grady

Memorial's mission statement and the phrase "compassionate" healthcare. In non-legal and non-financial terms, the reciprocity for the compassion is appreciation. Reciprocity comes from the recipient of the compassion. That is the patient who responds not only with a "thank you" but also with payment for services rendered by the person to whom the compassion was delivered. In legal and financial terms, this is called "consideration" and means, generally, payment.

Running parallel with the exchange described above is "privity of contract." While I was tempted to revisit my law school and dig up a terrific law review article that would serve as an eloquent discussion of the concept, it will serve our purpose to assert that a contract is between two parties and the only folks who can assert rights or obligations under the contract are the two parties that make up the contract. The elements of a contract are offer, acceptance, and an exchange of consideration. Sometimes, a third party has rights under the contract as a beneficiary to the contract between two other parties.

In healthcare, this model of privity between the parties in contract has been devastated. Why? Because there is no "true" privity of contract between the patient and provider. Consider who is the buyer and seller: the "buyer" is not actually the patient; the buyer is the insurance company. The price of care is determined for "in network" providers, who are in a contract with the insurance company, and the patient has limited rights in the contractual relationship regarding the cost of healthcare goods or services.

For example, except in New Hampshire, the patient does not own their own medical or healthcare data and cannot negotiate prices for care. In fact, a caregiver who allows a patient to pay an amount other than that mandated by the insurance company can be subject to civil and, potentially, criminal liability. At the same time, if an insured patient goes to the emergency room of a hospital covered by their insurance, the hospital can subcontract services to doctors, anesthesiologists, and other providers that are "out of network." Though such "outsourcing" translates into higher charges for the insurance company and the patient, the hospital does not need to tell the patient or the insurance company in advance of delivering treatment (or a bill) to the patient. However, the patient is, nonetheless, obligated to pay the bills from the in-network and out-of-network providers arising out of that emergency room visit, which can amount to tens of thousands of dollars.

The Heart of the Issue

This basic exchange between buyer and seller is not legal or conceptual philosophical gibberish but is at the heart of the problem with healthcare. Having a third party, the insurance company, pay for essential healthcare services changes the engagement between the caregiver providing services and the patient—the one who needs the care. It allows, though does not compel, the caregiver to become callous or indifferent to the patient's suffering. It also allows the caregiver to be less concerned about the sense of fairness in the exchange. To be clear, most healthcare providers are deeply mission-oriented people, but this conflict of interest challenges them all. So well-known is the conflict that it often appears in television shows and movies, which is why it remains puzzling as to why it has not been solved. Worse yet, the insurance company is not the only party intervening in the relationship between the parties. So, too, is the government (state, federal, and local), and let's not also forget the internal governance rules of the service provider themselves that also create conflicts.

I know a cardiologist whom I consider a good friend. He has been a cardiologist for a long time. He has provided care to extremely wealthy people and extremely poor people, and people of every level of income and wealth in between. In some instances where the patient was not insured or a participant in Medicaid or Medicare, he has taken chickens as payment, because that was what the patient could afford. He accepted those chickens with grace and care. He was compassionate both in providing the care and in receiving the currency (the chickens) with which the "bill" was paid. The cardiologist can make this decision himself. He's an independent contractor, not part of a network under contract to an insurance company. When he decides to accept fair payment, he does not have to process a claim, wait for sixty days to see if he is going to get paid, find out he is not going to get paid because the coding was "wrong," resubmit the claim, and then get paid sixty days after that. No, the cardiologist dealt directly with the patient, and the patient dealt directly with the cardiologist.

This is not to say that doctors should be paid with chickens. It is merely attempting to highlight that the relationship between the care provider and the patient must necessarily be anchored in compassion. In the context of this bilateral relationship, the introduction of an insurance carrier paying a part, or all of the bill makes it a "trilateral" relationship. We need to increase the instances where relationships are bilateral throughout the industry.

When the Insurance Company Pays, It Is Not Free

By their nature, insurance companies have intervened in the bilateral contract between patients and healthcare providers to take advantage of the exchange between patient and provider. The desire of the insurance companies was to make money, not a bad thing, but the way they make money is fundamentally tied to getting between the provider and the patient. What began as insurance to help avoid financial calamity arising out of a healthcare need has become a "lay-away" plan for healthcare. Instead of patients having the financial risk of paying for healthcare services rendered, insurance companies do. Instead of patients having the responsibility for their lifestyle choices, insurance companies do.

Patients have, through the insurance programs to which they have subscribed, diminished their financial liability for all major healthcare related financial issues to an operating expense paid monthly that calls for the least risk possible. Instead of paying, for example, $100 a month for a plan with a $10,000 deductible, they are paying $2,500 a month for a plan with a $250 deductible. So uncertain and gripped in fear of financial ruin have the individual and family become that they would rather figure out how to pay the significant monthly amount for fear that they MIGHT sometime have to pay the more sizeable deductible.

The delivery of compassion, meaning having both the understanding of the patient's problem AND having the desire to and the professional capability to solve the patient's problem, needs to find reciprocity in an expression of thanks that includes a verbal "thank you" coupled with payment. The exchange of service for compensation has to happen between two parties engaged in contract. Without the contemporaneous exchange, the model breaks down.

This direct relationship engages so much more than just money. The direct engagement also encourages greater information exchange—a process of education for the patient and the patient's family. If we do not achieve this redefinition of the nature of the healthcare industry as a separate entity from the insurance industry, Americans will know less about their healthcare and only become more dependent on a system whose interests are contrary to those of the patient.

When I discuss how others deal with healthcare problems, I find it fascinating to hear the responses:

"What was the problem?" I might ask. "How much did it cost to fix the problem?" "I don't know, the insurance company paid." "Did you look at the EOB (explanation of benefits)?" "No, I can never understand those things. Besides, it is not for me anyway because the insurance company pays the bill."

"What alternatives did you have?" "I am unsure," is the response. "How did you evaluate which course of action to take?" "I just did what the doctor told me to do."

And, of course, I never ask the question about doing a cost-benefit analysis given the risk profile of the alternatives.

"What?"

One common, though astonishing, remark I hear from healthcare professionals is that Americans are insufficiently educated to understand how to buy healthcare. In other words, they are too ignorant of the way the body works, the way that medicines work, the way that surgeries work, the way that anesthesia works, and the way that any alternative to medicine or surgery might work to understand their own healthcare needs or the cost of providing services to satisfy those needs. First, I disagree. Second, this would be the only industry in which that would be the case. Millions of consumers engage them every day, but how many folks understand artificial intelligence, bots, the difference between the internet and the web, how cell phones work, how the media industry works, or how to change their car's oil?

Instead, we use a proxy for making decisions where we might not know all the details of how something works. For example, few of us could now change the oil in our car. We see a light go on somewhere in the gauge cluster that means something needs to be checked. Sometimes, the light may be specific in telling the driver to change the oil in the car. Our response is not to change the oil ourselves but to take the car to someone who knows how to change the oil. The oil change provider will typically both post and quote a price and the car owner will ask questions, check prices with other service providers, evaluate the risk of using a discount provider rather than a dealer, and make a decision. The car owner will not question the service provider about paying his supplier for the oil used, the oil filter, or the labor. The car owner will not worry about getting a bill for supplies after the fact or getting a bill for an out-of-network filter removal specialist or a waste disposal service provider.

Privity of contract is the relationship between the buyer of goods or services and the seller of goods or services. For a buyer to enter into a contract, there is an assumption that the buyer and seller are on equal footing with regard to the negotiation of the contract and that the price they've agreed is fair for the goods or services purchased from the seller. Privity is the anchor to "consumerism" and "market forces."

We need a system that provides for more people with the financial capability to pay for services directly, thereby putting economic pressure on providers to improve quality and reduce price. Healthcare should be no different than any other industry in America. Imagine if the cost of healthcare had declined in a manner analogous to the decline in the costs of a computer chip or a flat-screen television: an obsolete HP 3000 with a fraction of the compute capability of a $500 smartphone today would cost $571,791 in inflation adjusted terms.[1] The marketplace has driven those costs down.

Privity of contract will lead to improved quality and decreased cost through increased consumerism. We have too little consumerism in making healthcare decisions either because we rely on government provided programs, like Medicaid or Medicare, or on insurance through a third-party carrier. The single, limited advancement toward consumerism was with the introduction of the Health Savings Account implemented under George W. Bush. The lack of consumerism in healthcare is another problem the 60% Solution seeks to solve.

Data, Data Everywhere but Not a Bit to Analyze

Another intertwined issue with privity of contract relates to healthcare data. First, who owns your medical data? Guess what, unless you live in New Hampshire, the answer is not you. That is right: the patient does not own their own medical data. The lab company, the imaging company, the hospital, the doctor, and whomever else collected that data owns the data. They can use that data for their purposes, selling it to marketing firms, service providers, and countless others in many instances. Under HIPPA, the acronym for the Health Insurance Portability Act containing many rules around patient privacy and personally identifiable medical data usage, there are supposed to be limitations as to what healthcare providers can do with a patient's records; however, the limits are insufficient. Alarming news reports have recently disclosed that Google and others have purchased personally identifiable medical data,[2] and there are other problems.

Recall the last time you checked in for a visit with a doctor or nurse. Someone behind a desk shoved a clipboard across the counter and told you to fill out and sign a bunch of documents. Included in those documents are permissions and releases. What happens if you don't sign them? Will you still be seen by the doctor or nurse? It depends. Failure to consent to certain releases or waivers may change the way the service is delivered or prevent the service from being delivered at all.

At the same time, consider the challenge of collecting all your medical information and getting it into one place. Back to the example of my mother, there was no way that anyone could have possibly remembered every injury, allergy, surgery, or other medical issue my mother had encountered during her life, particularly after the accident. How would one aggregate that into one digital location—what would one do with it if it could be aggregated?

Simply consider my mother's transition from Grady to Emory. Having someone quickly ingest all of that material collected during her months long stay in Grady was, itself, a big issue. My mother's medical records, all paper then, would have filled a room. Almost fifty years later, we still have not solved this problem today! Many doctors' offices continue to demand that records be sent to a fax machine because they don't trust email. Further, most practices don't combine or integrate these materials in anything other than a paper file folder.

Meanwhile, doctors and nurses are increasingly frustrated with the jobs they spent far too many years preparing for. Costly education, grueling hours, and looming financial and legal risk all lead to decreased patient interaction. Human gestures like eye contact have given way to staring at a screen to enter data soon after or even during the patient visit. Attention paid to completing a form distracts healthcare practitioners from giving attention to the human in front of them in a six-minute visit, the same human who they are reliant upon to understand or solve the problem at the center of their interaction. The compressed format of the visit prevents the practitioner from conveying concern or even interest and denies them the ability to see where further inquiry is warranted. The absence of human exchange serves to dehumanize the experience.

Calls for electronic health records or electronic medical records—and I have yet to find a doctor who can offer a consistent definition of either—are now being described as digital health biographies and regulations addressing the need to keep these records are also onerous and create risk for the caregiver or the custodian of records if they fail to keep the records as required by law. There is another problem: no one is aggregating the records in a single place. The patient is not aggregating records; in fact, the patient cannot physically or digitally aggregate the records. Frequently, the software systems used by different healthcare providers are incompatible. Even doctors in the same system won't get the records for procedures they did not perform, frequently because it would never occur for them to ask.

The general practitioner or primary care physician does not aggregate the records from other physicians or hospitals, despite the fact that the GP usually has to see the patient before referring the patient to a specialist. The specialist does not send his or her records back to the GP for aggregation. At the same time, the specialist does not send the record to the patient for aggregation.

This is not a technology problem; it is a market incentive problem. The lack of interoperability combined with the lack of industry or patient acceptance of a single application or an agreed set of application protocols that would allow the exchange and storage of these records coming from different providers using incompatible technologies encourages one to "stay within the system," thus discouraging transparency and competition. The "system" does not want healthcare records to be portable, does not want competition, and does not want costs to go down. As important as are "barriers to entry" to companies seeking to stifle competition, so to are "barriers to exit." In other words, there is a disincentive to leaving a systems or a clinician if you cannot take your medical records with you conveniently. Systems that cannot communicate with each other do exactly that, discourage, if not altogether prevent patients from taking their patient information to a new provider.

As a result, we have digitized the interaction that constitutes a doctor's visit, lab test, an X ray, an MRI, or a prescription. While digitizing records may be helpful, none of these digital interactions is forwarded to a single repository where a physician can review all of these interactions to understand what is going on with the patient's medical history. Worse, none of the information is stored by the patient and, worse yet—again—the patient does not even own their own information! In effect, the patient's experience of care is compromised in order to serve this digital data collection process, but the data is not managed in a way that can be leveraged to the patient's advantage in terms of healthcare outcomes. As important as are "barriers to entry" to companies seeking to stifle competition, so too are "barriers to exit." In other words, there is a disincentive to leaving a system or a clinician if you cannot take your medical records with you conveniently. Systems that cannot communicate with each other do exactly that: discourage, if not altogether prevent, patients from taking their patient information to a new provider.

This is one of the problems that The 60% Solution intends to solve, or at least make a lot better.

The Goals of this Book . . . Finally!

Stepping back into the reality of the healthcare industry and the subject of this book, my family dealt with a superset of the issues most families in the United States must deal with regarding the care of their loved ones. Our problems included the issues where insurance was involved, was not involved, and everything in between. However, I do not pretend for one minute that the anguish my family felt was more difficult, intense, insufferable, or painful than that of anyone else caring for their loved one. Anguish is just that, anguish. It is not relative or comparable from one person to another but rather a subjective experience of the person suffering the anguish.

Before moving on, it is important to note that these are my memories and experiences, and I am certain Berkeley and later, my stepsisters (Linda, Pam, and Diana) have their own versions of these memories. Each of us has our own perspective on our shared experience and time changes the speed, intensity, and recollection in these situations. One second of seeing a loved one in this condition feels like an eternity, an hour is more difficult yet, and repeating the experiences for years is more difficult than most can imagine. The anguish one feels in each instance is not greater or lesser than the anguish of another when their loved one is in pain or discomfort or distress.

And, that is the point.

The goal of this book is not to make every child and every child's mother happy. When a person, young, old or in between, needs medical attention, the first thing that person should think about is not whether the healthcare provider is in network, or whether the needed care is covered by insurance, or whether the insurance company will honor its obligation. Every administrative step should either be self-contained and not require further attention or be made easier so that patient and their loved ones can be relieved of additional stress and focus on the right thing: getting healthy.

It is the goal of this book to encourage the development of a compassionate healthcare industry. Compassion does not mean that care is free, nor does it mean that you get whatever you want, and it does not mean that someone else gets to decide for you. Compassion means an awareness of another's distress intertwined with a desire to relieve that person's pain or suffering.[3] To be specific, the doctor or hospital should be aware of the patient's distress and have a desire to relieve that pain or suffering. The many actors in this model are the doctor (or caregiver) and the patient. Notably absent is anything called an insurance company or the state government or federal government. No mention was made about in-network or out-of-network providers or claims to be processed. No! The relationship is between the caregiver and the patient.

Placing an insurance company between the caregiver and the patient it creates a state of confusion as to what duties are owed by whom to whom, what information is conveyed to whom, what payments are made by whom, and the healthcare exchange becomes unnecessarily cluttered and complex, producing many conflicts of interest between the two primary parties in contract: the caregiver and the patient. The same is true if we insert the government into the relationship between the caregiver and patient. Who gets to decide what care will or will not be provided by whom to whom?

To be unequivocally clear, it is bad to have an insurance company involved and the absolute worst thing that could ever happen to the US healthcare system is a single payor system. Such a system would be prohibitively expensive, permanently put a third and maybe fourth party between patient and caregiver, and lead to a less healthy society. Even Medicare, a program many claim is beloved by everyone over sixty-five, is economically unsound. According to an article in *The Federalist*, Medicare was originally expected to cost the United States $12 billion. The actual cost was $90 billion.[4] Today, it is projected to cost almost $1.5 trillion AND almost everyone with Medicare has either Part C or Part D, which are supplemental insurance plans to cover what Medicare does not cover!

Please do not assume that the problem this book is trying to solve is that of claims processing and recordkeeping. The problem this book is trying to solve is returning the relationship back to the parties in the contract: the doctor (or other caregiver) and the patient.

So, to recap, what problems are we trying to solve? Let's address and solve the impersonality of healthcare. Let's create an industry that embraces and manifests a compassionate healthcare delivery model. That means that caregivers identify a patient's problem and empathetically apply their professional training to address and resolve that patient's problem. Patients, family members, caregivers comprise the largest stakeholder group, and this is what they want. The real calling of caregivers to become caregivers is anchored in compassion. Compassion should be ubiquitous throughout the United States and the US healthcare industry. Caregivers should be free from the unnecessary administrative burdens of healthcare. Patients deserve to be treated by physicians they know and trust.

While we are at it, let's also improve availably,to and affordability of care. My firm, gTC Group, wrote the first ever Healthcare Inequality Index ("HII") that measured the availability and affordability of healthcare across the country by health service area (akin to a zip code around a hospital) in order to understand if services were available to those who could afford them in the corresponding jurisdiction. We found too many locations where there were either no services available or there were no affordable services available. We also found many instances where there were too many service providers and where services were available but not affordable. It should not come as a surprise that almost 300 hospitals have filed for bankruptcy since the Affordable Care Act ("ACA") was signed. Availability and affordability will both improve with market forces at work through consumerism.

Consumerism is not only about reducing cost. It is also about allocating responsibility among and between the participants in healthcare. We need to improve *both* patient *and* physician accountability. The lack of patient accountability arises, in part, out of the financial issue of payment. Why are Americans increasingly obese? What health problems are born out of poor eating, lack of exercise, and other variables controllable by the individual? Instead of taking responsibility for our own basic health needs, we use our lay-away plan for healthcare called insurance and happily embrace our co-dependence on the insurance company almost as though the insurance company were a parent of sorts. Personal responsibility cannot be under-emphasized any more than physician responsibility.

Consumerism will inevitably lead to a reduction of cost that permeates the system. Cost pressures will drive caregivers to get out of entrenched and archaic business processes (*e.g.,* communicating medical records through fax machines). Technologies will be implemented that have been available for years but have been reluctantly, if ever adopted, by the healthcare industry.

Consumerism will also fundamentally improve the exchange of information between the patient and doctor. This will lead to more informed patients making better decisions for themselves, rather than insurance companies getting poor information and making poor decisions for patients, like refusing to cover more than two MRIs in two years for a cancer patient. While the popular term for this is *transparency,* this term has lost some of its meaning. It is more often used to refer to pricing information. Pricing is part of transparency but only a part. The real meaning of transparency in the context of the healthcare exchange is a thorough discussion of the problem and the corresponding options for treatment.

Further, the reintroduction of consumerism in making healthcare choices will reduce fraud. Instead of gaming the system by employing professional coders who "code" the procedure in a way designed to yield the most revenue from the insurance company, the patient will pay the doctor directly and immediately. This will save the time value of money (doctors and hospitals frequently have accounts receivable that are well past 60 days, and it is not uncommon to have many accounts in excess of 90 or 120 days), thus improving cash flow for the entire industry. It will also reduce the cost of preparing claims as fewer will be produced, which will also reduce the legal liability for incorrectly (whether intentionally or unintentionally) coding claims.

Consumerism will also increase the number and nature of providers. Since the ACA was signed into law, provider oligopolies have formed in every metropolitan area in the United States. In Dallas, for example, three hospital systems comprise 91% of the market. Add the fourth largest system and the four combined comprise 98% of the market. And, it is no different on the payor side. Five insurance companies dominate the Dallas market. Why did this occur? Insurance companies want ubiquity of coverage: the greater the geographic coverage and the greater the number of services offered, the better! The same is true in reverse. The systems prefer fewer payors to deal with, as this cuts down on administrative costs and allows for greater familiarity between those in an increasingly small community of executives invested with the understanding of "how things work."

The sum of these problems has been coming for a long time. For those of us close enough to see it coming, the car is gaining speed and we have people interested in stripping away the brakes. We are an aging population with over 10,000 people a day moving on to Social Security and qualifying for Medicare.[5] We have an opioid problem, an obesity problem, a cancer problem, and countless other problems that are individually and collectively taxing an already compromised healthcare system. Remember, neither the federal government nor any state government actually provides healthcare services. For those who qualify, they merely pay for it. When they do, they make demands no one likes and produce outcomes no one likes.

It is not too late. We can change this. We must change this. Here is the really good news! The 60% Solution builds on existing laws, regulations, and models. No new paradigm has to be created for The 60% Solution to be adopted or for its benefits to be realized. No new companies have to be created. Patients win, caregivers win, and the other stakeholders win.

Chapter One
THE 60% SOLUTION

H. Ross Perot was working as a salesman for IBM in 1962, and he'd sold 100 percent of his full year quota in January, the first month of the year. The computers he sold were expensive computers meant for large companies. These were mainframe computer systems, behemoths by today's standards. He theorized that the typical schedule for which these computers would be used would be from 9 to 5. That meant for each of his customers there were roughly sixteen hours a day five days a week of unused, very expensive, compute capacity in the computers he sold. His first big idea was to lease that compute capability to other companies. Through countless iterations, this concept led to the development of what we know today as a the "outsourcing industry," a segment of the "business services" industry. Mr. Perot left IBM and created a company he called Electronic Data Systems Corporation (known later as "EDS") where he made a bunch of money. He later sold EDS to GM and made a bunch more money. Then, he created Perot Systems and made even more money before he sold Perot System to Dell and made even more money.

Through this process of business creation and development, Mr. Perot and his leadership team created great companies over many decades. One could argue that the approach taken by Mr. Perot in each instance was merely an incremental change to the business model before it. For example, renting machine capacity that was not fully utilized 100% of the time was not a new concept. Companies rented or leased cars, locomotives, mills, and other things that were capital intensive.

Wrapping business services around unused compute capability and thereby making the systems more operationally or economically efficient by taking advantage of that expanded comput capability was also not dissimilar to established business models. Make no mistake, though, inside each version of a Perot company, there was terrific insight, passion, culture, and innovation. However, Mr. Perot's companies did not seek to turn the world upside down and were in many ways very conservatively run firms that steadily created billions in value by thinking incrementally.

Thinking differently can produce outcomes that dwarf Mr. Perot's remarkable impact. Mind you, I am a big fan of Mr. Perot and the impact he has had on not only business, but on many other aspects of life. His genius should be celebrated, and his many achievements, many of which are not broadly known, should be applauded. However, from strictly a business perspective, when one considers what happened when Steve Jobs returned to the helm as Apple's CEO in 2000—entire industries would be changed:

The launch of the iPod in 2001 changed the music industry.

The launch of the iPhone in 2007 would change the telecom industry, the photography industry, the video industry.

The launch of the iPad in 2010 would change the computer industry and influence all media industry in all formats.

The launch of the Apple Watch changed the timekeeping industry, impacted the healthcare industry and, again, changed the computer industry.

Mr. Jobs did something very different than everyone else in the industry at that time. He thought about the problem of accessing content, whether it was a text file, a music file, or a video file, differently. He thought of each of these elements as part of an ecosystem. In other words, he took a "systems view" of the problem he was trying to solve. Apple is now valued at just under $2 trillion, a number that is so large as to be incomprehensible. The human brain cannot understand what $1 trillion actually is.

Jobs adopted the phrase "Think Different" as Apple's slogan in 1997, but he'd actually been thinking differently all his life. He employed systems thinking. Rather than think about hardware or software or services as individual, discreet offerings, he looked at the individual elements collectively as part of a system. In fact, under Jobs, "Apple's systems thinking grew to include the integration of products, services, content, distribution, communications, and developers—the creation of ecosystems."[1]

While working for EDS, these ideas about systems thinking took root in me and others in our industry and informed me in each of my learning relationships, my mentoring relationships, and in each of my leadership roles—though not always or consistently or perfectly. An idea that came from it which I continue to try to employ to this day, almost twenty-five years later, is that when I approach a problem, more than one solution is developed, each from a different way of thinking.

With this in mind, I sat down to think about healthcare in the context of my professional and personal experiences. I was keen to look at the industry as a system and to see if there was a different way to think about industry based on asking different questions:

What parts of the healthcare system were linked to each other?

How were they linked to each other?

Where were the things that needed to be turned upside down or rearranged or were altogether broken?

How could incentives and culture be better aligned?

Rather than thinking of healthcare as the responsibility of just the doctor or just the patient, what if we aggregated and integrated all of the elements of the healthcare exchange into something we could call a healthcare system? At the very least, we need to think about patients' needs and expectations in a common context with doctors, nurses, education, data, billing, accounting, information technology, regulations, supply chains, distribution models, research, and other elements to change healthcare. Just as Steve Jobs demonstrated with Apple, we need to think more broadly, inclusively, and collaboratively.

You might then ask, why is it called The 60% Solution? The answer is because reimagining and improving the 60% on which we are focused will necessarily and beneficially impact the rest of the system. The approach articulated within this book will provide a framework for moving from the current situation, which is almost uniformly regarded as just short of a disaster, to something that serves America's healthcare needs well.

The desperately needed changes in our healthcare system that are so hotly debated in Washington influence every interaction between the individual patient and a healthcare provider. Politicians want to solve the complexity of healthcare with more regulation, which will further limit market forces from working. This is counterproductive, expensive, unhealthy, and stunting.

The reactive, patchwork nature of the state and federal regulations that make up our current healthcare system is an outgrowth of the way our system has developed over centuries, and the increased pace of technological change has increased speed and momentum of new regulatory efforts over the last eight decades. The result today is an entanglement of outdated mandates, too many special interests with too much influence, and blurred lines between state and federal actions and responsibilities rendering cost-effective, high-quality, accessible healthcare impossible.

Just like the search for most solutions, and as is the case with most industries, we do not start with a fully designed end state in mind. A difference with healthcare is that we have quelled the forces of consumerism and at same time handcuffed the industry with regulation. The unsurprising result is an industry so large that even small percentages of corruption, properly, produce headline making, attention grabbing news involving enormous sums of money.

What generally happens in industry is entrepreneurs and innovators identify market needs and set about trying to meet them. They will land on an idea and introduce it to the marketplace. In response, purchasers of the goods and services put forward into the marketplace by these entrepreneurs and innovators unavoidably and beneficially shape the features, functions, and benefits of those products and services by the choices they make, including the prices that consumers will or won't pay for the goods and services offered by the industry. Occasionally, products or services are developed and become so perfectly refined that no further adjustments are needed, but this is rare. In most instances, products and services change because the nature of demand from purchasers changes or some exogenous factor compels changes. Previous generations often bought goods with an expectation of lasting excellence and application, today the constant need for something newer, better, or simply different has forced products and services into perpetual cycle of change and updates.

There are countless examples of this in healthcare. X-ray imaging has been supplemented with or replaced by MRIs, CT scans, or newer forms of imaging. Physicians must be educated on how these new technologies can be used, what technology it augments or replaces and why, the cost of using the technology, and what price the market will pay to benefit from the use of the technology. The market is created with certain specifications for the expectations of the imaging technology to be used and under what circumstances and what price will be paid. Meanwhile, innovators are working feverishly behind the scenes to make the technology better, faster, cheaper, and more ubiquitously adopted to feed the constant need to provide the latest and greatest.

Industries, and businesses within those industries, have a number of interested parties who collectively affect the operation of the industry. Customers, employees, independent contractors, suppliers, investors, lenders, governments (including state, local, and federal), and others all contribute to the operations of the business. The result is that to solve the riddle of healthcare one needs to think of these players as parts of a system where something that affects any affects all. regulations are particularly insidious with their reach across entity and organizational lines.

Any consideration of healthcare regulation starts by recognizing that there are in fact two forms of regulation: commercial and governmental. Commercial regulation comes in the form of the insurance companies developing plans and supporting models that include or exclude the use of new technology and establishing the corresponding prices patients must pay for those plans. In thirty-one states in the United States, those plans are then presented for approval by governmental regulators at the state Department of Insurance, but this state-level approval level is not really the second layer of regulation to which I earlier referred.

The second layer of regulation is more "top-down" in nature. meaning that a state or federal legislator is made aware of part of a problem, usually attached to a much broader and more complex issue, and sooner or later that legislator leads the charge to create a "solution" that only addresses the problem about which he or she has been made aware. This pattern of issue-oriented problem-solving ignores the full context of the initial offending problem, equally ignoring any resulting complications that pop up from the solution itself. This is the legislative equivalent of playing "Whack-a-Mole." In other words, the industry and its stakeholders are not regulated simply by consumer driven rules or even insurance driven rules, but rather by a latticework of "problem-specific solutions" each of which is developed by well-intentioned, elected officials and their bureaucratic colleagues in the agencies charged with rule-making and enforcement, neither of whom want to fail in re-election or be fired should their solutions prove ineffective or worse.

As a result, these governmental mandated, regulatory "solutions" are not simply myopic, they invite or even create a need for additional regulation. Just as a product or service will evolve, so too does the regulatory framework. (Note that we now produce over 100,000 pages of new laws, rules, and regulations at the federal level alone . . . each year!) Further, complying with these regulations is expensive, and that cost drives consolidation of industry players. Worse yet, the regulations create, strengthen, or even embolden economic stakeholders, which then become more powerful and entrenched.

Our current healthcare disaster is a broken vessel of outdated, leftover, and no longer useful ideas that limps along as our citizens become impaled by piercing financial demands and threats of financial devastation. Patients are terrorized by physicians or insurance companies who characterize their particular medical condition as "catastrophic."

While the nature of the threat posed by our current healthcare system is seemingly medical, the real threat the current healthcare system poses is the financial burden imposed by care rather than our system's ability to address the clinical care needs of the individual patient. The provision of healthcare in our country is extraordinary. We have access to the best minds, procedures, and medical answers that money can buy, And that is precisely the problem. We have no reluctance to throw big money after any solution for any healthcare problem which is why waste is so often overlooked or missed.

The Journal of the American Medical Association recently published a multi-year study showing that a staggering $245 billion dollars is currently being *wasted* in our healthcare delivery each year. That amounts to $1 of every $4 being spent is utterly wasted.[2] You can only imagine the shockwaves that entrenched stakeholders will feel when these excesses and waste are finally addressed, which they must be for our individual and collective financial futures to be viable. These industry stakeholders will inevitably resist any change that can make an impact. Insurance companies in particular will revolt.

Bloomberg News recently reported that the average cost of family coverage for health insurance has now reached a record high, topping the $20,000 per year mark.[3] Take that in for just a moment.

The 60% Solution encourages, if not rests on, helping the individual be or become financially capable, educated, and engaged in making their own healthcare decisions by activating and relying on the individual's power as a consumer to contribute positively to controlling the rising cost of the delivery of healthcare. At the center of this solution lies CHOICE.

- Financially capable means that individual consumers have sources of payment, whether through cash in their bank account, cash in an HSA, through public or private health insurance, or otherwise.

- Educated means that consumers have the opportunity to learn about and understand their own healthcare needs and options for care, with resources being available so they can effectively partner with a healthcare team to address their healthcare needs and options within the range of their available resources.

- Engaged means that patients are observing, listening, and considering their current situation and are prepared to act in their own best interests.

Consumer choice will drive market forces that compel the introduction of new technologies and mandate the elimination of waste. The goal of this plan is to genuinely reduce the cost of healthcare for everyone and thereby make healthcare more accessible. Most healthcare problems are solved by getting the care one needs, and this is not in any way an attempt to tell physicians how to practice medicine or how hospitals should extend their reach. This Solution simply seeks to make healthcare affordable and accessible to more people, but to be clear and with only a little hyperbole, *no one in the current industry has an economic interest in reducing the cost of healthcare!* The Solution begins by addressing the functions within the industry whose improvement will create the biggest beneficial impact for the greatest number of interested parties and the least adverse impact on patients throughout the industry. These include pricing, payment, and prevention. I consider these elements to be the "major muscles" in the Solution.

The Five Components of This Solution Are Meant to Be Comprehensive and Are Interdependent

Just as you do not start the swing of a baseball bat with your thumb, you don't transform healthcare by reengineering the registration process or some other single point of contact (aka "thumb") with the problem.

The five components of The 60% Solution are:

1. Emphasize Primary Care

Currently, how we seek, activate, and use primary care is most often dictated by the individual's insurance policy. At best, all parties involved in the healthcare exchange see the designation of a primary care provider as an unnecessary complication that separates the patient/consumer from their end goal of seeing a specialist, but that way of thinking is one of the dysfunctions that has developed over decades of impractical approaches to healthcare.

Most of us do not use primary care in the right way, and the tax code—until the very recent change—often discourages us from using primary care physicians. Creating more primary care physicians and equipping them with broader education and greater use of technology would allow more health issues to be addressed earlier, interrupting the need for specialists or advanced care and hospital visits. Most policies currently cover an annual checkup, but by having these performed by doctors with a broader range of medical understanding, we can identify and prevent more significant (and more costly) medical problems from emerging. Primary care physicians can better guide patients on the use of over-the-counter medications, preventive care options, and lifestyle choices we are making. Some estimate that this initiative to broaden the impact of primary care alone may create savings of almost $67 billion a year.[4]

By using a systems thinking approach to unfold the often mismatched and ill-fitting pieces of the healthcare puzzle, the 60% Solution examines how those pieces can better fit together and how each impacts the other. It is important note that the state of healthcare delivery in our country is functionally sound; it is the economic inefficiency of how the system operates that is the focus of the investigation of this book and is at the heart of the solution presented and argued, because it is the economics of the system that imperil the system's ability to provide better care.

2. Standardize Accounting and IT

As with every other industry, technology infuses a mix of simplification and complexity that constantly imposes a gritty, inflexible cadence to advancement. The foundation of healthcare is shifting to include more technology, but many in the industry still do not understand technology and how invasive it is, permeating every aspect of healthcare. The perception that information technology is merely a tool for streamlining administrative functions of healthcare, like billing or payments, is neither fair nor more accurate than asserting that IT is merely a set of tools for aggregating individual medical records into a combined sum of separate reports over time.

It may seem strange to link the profession and practices of accounting and information technology, but they are remarkably interdependent in most industries and particularly so in the healthcare industry. Simply tracking the complex web of diagnostic, treatment, and service codes that make up the tenth revision of the International Classification of Diseases and Related Health Problems ("ICD-10") requires an enormous, integrated database and more computing capability than existed on the lunar module that landed on the moon.

Information technology is merely a set of tools that can do some or all the things needed to manage and provide care efficiently. To decide what information technologies will be employed to do this and how it will be best done is the product of thousands of decisions that every stakeholder in the industry should contribute to making. The challenge is that few of us have the patience or discipline to go through all those questions and contribute to those decisions or to understand the intended and unintended consequences of those decisions.

Regulations Matter

Few pieces of legislation have been more impactful in healthcare in the last twenty years than the Health Insurance Portability and Accountability Act, or HIPAA, passed in 1996 and the Health Information Technology for Economic and Clinical Health Act, or the HITECH Act, passed in 2009.

HIPAA made certain that individuals could retain their health insurance if they moved from one employer to another or if, for any reason, the individual stopped working. HIPAA also directed the Department of Health and Human Services ("HHS") to create rules governing the protection of patient information and implement standards regarding the electronic transmission of patient information.

The HITECH Act was created to encourage use of electronic health records ("EHRs") throughout the healthcare industry. It also created a set of incentives and penalties related to compliance with the obligations set forth under the Act.

Less clear, however, was what an EHR was and how it differed from another poorly defined term, the electronic medical record or EMR. Our examination of this component in chapter 4 addresses the primary complexities in the administration and application of these two Acts. The many gaps between these two critical legislative initiatives call out for standardization, and specific recommendations are presented.

The HITECH Act incented adoption of information technology but was not prescriptive. Administrators were left to implement technology or deal with the financial and regulatory consequences of failing to do so. Despite providing limited or insufficient input, physicians grew angry and are now very dissatisfied with their newfound job requirements. So demanding are the systems, that doctors and patients now complain that there is virtually no eye contact between patient and physician during a visit, as the physician is all too occupied entering information into the "system."[5]

People invariably think that technology is the solution or AI is the solution, but few actually understand that both of these potential solutions are merely codifications of logic by someone making decisions on how things are supposed to work. For example, in today's parlance, let's imagine that a patient has a heart problem and enters the hospital with chest pains and while in the hospital, the patient has a heart attack. Tests show that the patient is overweight, has coronary artery blockage from high cholesterol, and has COVID-19. Artificial intelligence, or AI, has logic written into the software code that will provide an answer to what is causing the patient's problem. However, the software is not necessarily smarter or dumber than the attending physicians, rather it is simply using a different set of logic statements and working with a predetermined set of values that have been assigned to each factor. If the patient dies from the heart attack, what will be the cause of death? Would it be different if the patient was forty years old rather than seventy years old? How would an age of fifty impact the coding compared to an age of sixty? By blindly looking to technology alone humans are merely outsourcing these decisions to software code based on a set of criteria that may or may not be correct, which is necessarily informed by the science and accepted approaches of the time, but which is incapable of adding greater understanding of the patent as a whole.

The inputs into the system primarily serve to inform costs structures and billing systems, such as a general ledger, a charge master, a balance sheet, an income statement, and cashflow statements. These will go on to influence payments by patients and insurance companies, which will inform decisions about what doctor or system will provide treatment, and for how long, and will further influence the medical and financial aspects of the care plan. All of which greatly affects the "whole" human being receiving care, but does not directly affect the outcomes that patient experiences as a result.

To take one example, insurance companies do not pay hospitals on a "fee for service" basis. Instead, insurance companies pays the hospital a percentage of the "gross billed charges." As that percentage has remained fairly constant, insurance companies are, in essence, encouraging hospitals to inflate the gross billed charges by increasing the number of services and provider/patient interactions while the patient is in the hospital, thus causing the private insurance companies to subsidize the hospitals by encouraging them not to focus on reducing costs. More specifically, hospitals typically bill about 3.5 times more than they collect.

This conflict of interests creates problems that touch on virtually every aspect of payment, all the way through to the insurance company CEO's compensation. A public company CEO is compensated with a base salary, bonus, and benefits, but the real money usually comes from the stock options (or their equivalent) that allow the CEO to benefit from the increase in the stock price that occurs during the CEO's tenure.

Market forces evident in other industries are also subject to barriers. Technology brings this into sharp relief by exposing the antiquated, geography-based notion of professional licensing models. Although you may think the next issue is that of allowing insurance companies to sell policies across state lines, the problem is more basic than that. Doctors, nurses, radiologists, and most everyone else in the US healthcare industry requiring licenses are licensed by the state in which they practice. So, how then do we address the issues and opportunities of telemedicine? How do we use videoconferencing technologies to access healthcare resources from smartphones while we're in transit or through a computer at the patient's home or office? Even if you solve the licensing issue, other issues arise. If the patient is harmed, which state's tort laws apply? If the bill is coded improperly such that it gives rise to potential criminality, which state's criminal laws apply? There is an urgency to get standards in place as technology advances and the resulting implications only become more complex as even the most basic issues remain resolved.

One excellent example of a game changer in healthcare is the system of ICD-10 codes that dictates what will be covered by third-party payors and at what level of reimbursement. Patients' entire financial futures and access to the best care rests on the proper assignment of these codes. While humans make decisions about which codes are applied, once the codes are entered, everything else is automated. Despite having regulations compelling the use of electronic health records and other forms of mandated technology and the imposition of substantial fines on those who don't, the HITECH Act has failed miserably in reaching its goal of using technology to reduce the cost of healthcare. Yes, adoption rates of electronic records have increased, but *to this day* we still fax health records because of HIPAA concerns over the security of email. Yes, we have amassed tremendous volumes of data, but it is clear that patients do not own their data in 49 of 50 states[6] and the data is less likely to be comprehensively consumed for healthcare decisions and much more likely to be comprehensively consumed for marketing decisions.

The key issue is that the industry lost the notion of the patient as the "customer." Instead, the customer may be the physician, the insurance company, the employer, or any of a number of other actors in the ecosystem. The easy way to identify the customer is to identify who is paying the bills. Again, the payor is not the customer here, and that disconnection creates a domino effect of problems, partial solutions, regulations, workarounds, and distress. No aspect of our current delivery model is patient-centric. In chapter 4 you will discover standardization recommendations that will give a clear view of how standardized accounting and technology best serve the patient by creating patient-centric healthcare. How can any patient feel empowered without control, access, and choice?

3. Clarify Pricing

A challenge that you may find interesting is to ask any care provider you see what the price is of the service needed. The more complex the need, the more challenging quoting a price is, if the doctor even knows. When I have asked the question in the past, the response has ranged from anger at my even asking such a question to disbelief that I cared. I once was told my mother had to move from a hospital to "rehab" after having pneumonia. I asked why and was told she needed to "build up her strength." When I asked how much that would cost, their answer was, "Why do you care? It is free under Medicare."

Today, if I were to ask a doctor the cost of a knee replacement, he or she would not be able to answer the question. Even if you ask the cost of a single prescription or of a simple procedure, I think you are likely to find that no one can give you an accurate answer. There is a reason for that, and it stems from the many layers of ancillary services and charges that get piled on top of what it actually costs to provide a service.

In an even more timely and frustrating example of this problem, I had a visit with my doctor where a blood test was required. The date of the visit was June 11, and the date of the explanation of benefits, or EOB, that I received was about forty-five days later. The EOB was sent by regular mail, and included eight pieces of paper, six of which had print on both sides, some in a variety of languages. On the first page, sixteen lines of the page were dedicated to the explanation of benefits, meaning how much was charged by the doctor, how much was charged by the lab company, how much was paid by the insurance company to each of the doctor and the lab services company, and how much I had to pay as the remainder. Just to be clear, the actual explanation of benefits was sixteen lines on one page. There was plenty of blank space on the page.

So, what were the remaining pages for? Five of the printed pages were dedicated to an explanation of HIPAA and privacy practices. This was referenced above, and while well-meaning, has invaded every aspect of every interaction between provider, payor, and patient. The remaining two printed pages were dedicated to an explanation of how to file an appeal, including details regarding what information was required, by whom, within what time frame, to whom the appeal should be sent, and what would happen through the course of the appeals process. All of this is because we have no clearly stated prices and it is complicated to determine who is supposed to pay what, coupled, of course, with each of the players in the drama having an economic incentive to pay the least possible amount they can pay. When we consider that the patient is paying the insurance company monthly in advance, it becomes apparent that there is a wildly asymmetric balance of power in favor of the insurance company with all of its concomitant resources. Insurance companies are big, have many rules, lawyers to enforce those rules and defend against those challenging the insurance companies or their rules, and they have already received your payment. Your attempts to get the service to which you are entitled are met with a singular promise: it will cost you time and more money.

Thus, it constantly amazes that no one providing healthcare services can tell you the price of most services. Pricing is currently determined by complicated algorithms that rely on increasingly endless variables. The Solution rests on every service and procedure having a price that can be published and understood and the patient in partnership with their healthcare provider having the ability to incorporate that knowledge in making healthcare choices. Information technology was supposed to help with this, but the power structure of consumer choice has been stripped from patients through the complexity of the system, and this has created vulnerabilities and dependencies that have removed buying power from the consumer.

Our healthcare choices are currently dictated by doing the best we can to grasp what we're up against in any given situation, usually at times when we are our most stressed and feeling most vulnerable. Why do any of us subject ourselves to that victim mentality? Because it is the reality of having to make decisions without having access to real prices for the essential care we need. Imagine being given an itemized statement of the various procedures you need. Most of us today would never enter any financial arrangement without a very clear understanding of the pricing, cost, and responsibility to pay.

The opacity however, does not end there. Government incentives to businesses and patients add to the complexity of understanding pricing in its entirety. In other words, government incentives create discounts that hide the true costs of healthcare. These discounts come in the form of tax treatments, mandates, regulations and other difficult to find or understand interventions.

For example, most of us don't realize that we still live under the tax impacts of economic decisions that were made during World War II. The Stabilization Act and the Revenue Act of 1942 were the first codification of the tax treatment of benefits for the employer and employee. During the war, employers were prevented from raising wages beyond capitations set forth by the federal government; however, there was an exemption for healthcare benefits in the form of insurance that allowed businesses to declare the benefit as a tax deduction and the employee to not be taxed on the receipt of the benefit. Mind you, at this time in our history, the US population was about 135 million—less than half of what it is today—with only 10 percent of that population having health insurance. The unemployment rate was 4.7% that year and would fall to 1.2% in 1944, the lowest in recorded history. (Virtually everyone was in the labor force, and the unemployment calculation included everyone over ten years old!) The federal government had a public policy interest in getting workers healthcare (and getting them back to work), businesses suffered high tax rates with some paying a rate of 90% on profits over a certain threshold. However, this tax incentive to provide health insurance also disempowered the employee by reassigning market power to the insurance companies and eliminating consumer knowledge about the costs of healthcare services. The effects of this practice have carried forward in different iterations now for almost eight decades. The problem is now astonishingly larger as the US population is now more than 330 million and approximately 80 percent of Americans now have health insurance. The approach I propose will finally re-introduce the benefits of consumerism into our healthcare choices and bring myriad benefits to the entire US economy.

4. Change Governance

It was 1910 when the biggest seismic event in the history of medicine took place. It had nothing to do with a medical discovery, an invention of any kind, a new protocol, or anything having to do with a clinic, a doctor, a patient, a disease, a test, or a surgical procedure. Rumor has it that the protagonist to this historical change was a racist, a bigot, and a chauvinist who was "paid off" by the American Medical Association to protect its membership from competition. The Solution does not particularly care if those accusations are true, but it does care to deal with the aftermath of poor quality, great expense, uneven availability, and limited understanding that have been the result.

Abraham Flexner was not a doctor or a scientist, and he graduated from college in two years—something pointed out often by his critics. However, he was an educator funded by the Carnegie Foundation to perform a study of medical schools in the United States and Canada. His findings were released in 1910 in a report not-so-surprisingly called the Flexner Report. The underlying premise of the report was that medicine needed to be anchored in science that was supported by the empirical method. In Flexner's view, this premise revealed that the overwhelming majority of "medical schools" were in fact incapable of, or even uninterested in, training physicians this way. The result of his findings was a wholesale change in the way in which doctors were educated and licensed across the United States and Canada.

Flexner's findings and recommendations would also extend to all types of caregivers, from medical doctors to osteopathic doctors to chiropractors to nurses to dentists to hygienists to rehab specialists and others. Flexner asserted that doctors should be required to first attend undergraduate school (meaning four years of college coursework) and then attend four years of medical school, which would ideally be followed by several additional years spent in internships, residencies, and fellowships.

Many existing medical schools either reformed or closed. Others modified their curricula to comply with Flexner's recommendations. Notwithstanding the historically recent advent of undergraduate and graduate school scholarships, the cost alone of being able to get through eight years of higher education was and remains both daunting and largely reserved for sons and daughters of wealthy parents and top students who through almost super-human efforts are able to obtain scholarships or are willing and able to assume enormous levels of personal debt to fund their education. The actual cost borne by medical students is two-fold. The student has to pay to go to school, and because of the demands of the training and study, the student cannot work while going to school. In other words, money is going out while no money is coming in . . . for the better part of at least eight years. Menial wages paid during internships and residencies, which are still insufficient to pay all of the bills much less to catch up on fees already owed, follow years of study.

Additionally, the educational rigor, added to the cost, created, and continues to create tremendous barriers to entry into the field of medicine. From a competition perspective, the barriers are only made worse by state licensing laws that require prospective doctors to take exams one would likely only pass if the applicant had completed the required course of study. In addition, the percentage of those taking the exams who pass, even after the completion of the educational requirements, remains less than, but close to, 100%, thus calling into question the value or need for the exams themselves. In other words, an aspiring medical student must graduate from an accredited school to take the state's licensing exam, and they must pass the exam to be licensed to practice medicine, which begs the question of the value of the medical school's accreditation. If you graduate from the accredited school, why does one have to take an additional test? Further, if a student can pass the test without going to an accredited school what is the value of the accreditation? The answer is that both requirements are artificial disincentives to trying and barriers to entry.

Flexner's findings had racial implications also. Flexner has been quoted as saying that blacks should not be allowed to practice medicine in white communities because blacks would expose whites to diseases to which whites had no or could not develop immunity. Remember, Flexner was not a doctor or a scientist nor was there a study cited in his quote! In fact, in the years following the release of his report, five of the seven historically black medical schools in the country closed, leaving only Meharry Medical College in Nashville and Howard University College of Medicine in Washington, D.C. This long reach of Flexner continues today, as blacks comprise approximately 13 percent of the population of the United States while comprising only about 4 percent of the physician population. It is notable too that 80 percent of those 4 percent are graduates from one of those two schools: Meharry or Howard.

The Solution recommends changing the undergraduate curricula, the graduate curricula, and licensing requirements for medical professionals. Not only would this reduce barriers and attract more applicants to the healthcare professions, it would provide greater opportunities to distribute healthcare services and make them more affordable.

5. Modify HSAs

With a greater quantity and diversity of healthcare providers, ideally distributed more broadly across the United States, equipped with better information technology delivering services with clear prices supported by better accounting rules, the question remains, "How can we drive change from the current system that is so reliant on insurance to a consumer-driven model?" Further, given the tax code has been used consistently to incent behavior, and for healthcare purposes could actually both incent health while reducing future state and federal expenditures, health savings accounts, or "HSAs," are a good tool with which we can expand the affordability of healthcare.

Placing consumerism at the forefront of this proposal opens the door for HSAs to do the heavy lifting of moving families out of the financial duress caused by health demands. The seminal work done by John Goodman and his colleagues at the National Center for Policy Analysis and, later, at the Goodman Institute created what we now call the Health Savings Account or HSA. While this creates a tax advantaged way for people to save for their healthcare needs, it has by itself, as I am certain Dr. Goodman would agree, does not go far enough in providing the needed changes to instill the employee with market power and market knowledge. More importantly, HSAs are currently only available to those who can afford to take advantage of them, creating a financial chasm between those leaving Medicaid and households with a gross income of 300% of the federal poverty level or "FPL." Indexing benefits from governmental entities into HSAs held by those from 150% of FPL to 300% of FPL will result in creating more consumers who are able to exert market power on the industry, and that will allow this stratum of the US population to benefit in many important ways that will have a domino effect for every other participant in the industry.

The goals of this Solution are to reduce the cost of healthcare for all and to help lift many out of poverty. The former helps the latter, but it also helps everyone participating in the economy. The latter helps not only the people who are currently working or poor, but it also seeks to help the families of those working or poor. While everyone will benefit from this plan, I admit that the wealthy will benefit less and less directly. However, the wealthy who are business owners may benefit more. Neither of these outcomes is inherently bad. Similarly, individuals of all economic means will benefit by knowing what their costs for essential care will be and enjoying lower costs in the aggregate.

The seminal and overarching meta-principle of The Solution is that all attributes, elements, processes, and tools in the delivery of and payment for healthcare should be developed and should advance the goal of creating and supporting a consumer-based relationship between the patient and each caregiver.

All of the tools exist today to make this a reality, though some of them may need a little "change" or "tweak." Together, we need to encourage political leaders, technology companies, and caregivers to champion the changes advocated in subsequent chapters, which address where we are today, how we got here, and how to move forward from here to a better healthcare model in the future. You will note that there is a chapter addressing the future of healthcare entitled "The Very Near Future of Healthcare." The reason for that is my belief that we can get there soon. This is not a vision that must take a generation to achieve but one which we must push to achieve as quickly as possible.

Chapter Two
EMPHASIZE PRIMARY CARE

All of the insurance in the world will not prevent health problems. Insurance may give you access; it may encourage you to do more if certain costs are covered; and it contributes to early detection and hopefully treatment for developing problems. Ultimately, our own good health relies on each of us something good for ourselves, which is also doing something good for all of us. When we take care of ourselves, we are doing a service for the community. Another way of looking at it is that when you take care of yourself, you favorably affect the pool being insured, thus improving the costs for everyone. This has implications for all costs related to care, including Medicare, Medicaid, prescription drugs, food, and other costs.

The important thrust of the 60% Solution is to move greater control, responsibility, and choice about healthcare options to the individual so that each can make good decisions. Ancillary to this empowerment of the individual, as is the case with industries other than healthcare, is that individuals, families, and communities separately and collectively "learn."

Assume for the moment that access to parks contributes to improved health for those who live near a park. Having access to a park would then be a public good, and cities should want to create and maintain parks for their residents. For a city to create a park and agree to maintain that park, a group of people needs to collectively agree in the civic project of creating and maintaining a park. While there are many good reasons for parks, you, as an individual, must conclude that improving the health of the community is a good enough reason for creating a park. Others would need to share that belief before the park is created, so when that park is created, it reflects the conclusion of many people who have learned one way or another that parks contribute to the health of the community.

Now, some readers will be stultified by the obvious conclusion that parks are good for health, while others may find this a novel idea . . . even today. The point is about how we collectively learn over time. For us to collectively learn, we must individually learn until enough individuals reach a tipping point of collective agreement.

This brings us back to healthcare. We need to individually and collectively learn more and learn more rapidly about what contributes to and detracts from our individual and collective health. To learn, information flow must be open, direct, clear, and easy to understand. Impediments to learning, therefore, are contrary to the goal of individual and collective learning about healthcare.

The first part of this chapter will address what is important for the individual to know and do for themselves in a very direct way. The second part of the chapter is going to define primary care and make recommendations about how to effectively engage with your primary care provider and what you should demand of your primary care provider. Then, I will close with thoughts and data that give some insights into how to best pay for primary care.

For Your Own Best Health

The first step is doing what few want to hear, read, or talk about. This step includes taking actions and developing habits that are very basic and, though everyone may have been told about them, too few of us follow the guidance : eat well, get seven or more hours of sleep each day, and engage in regular exercise.

Critics assert that such recommendations are easy to make if you have plenty of time, live in the right neighborhood, have access to good food, are affluent, not a parent, not a single parent, or not old. While I believe those arguments are both inaccurate and hyperbolic, I do understand that no one will eat right every day, sleep well every night, or get the right type of exercise for the right amount of time every day. Each of us has a number of competing interests and demands on our time that may make this difficult on any given day. Caring for children, caring for parents, work, and other of life's challenges and obligations get in the way. However, even against busy schedules and challenging finances, most of us, with effort, can reach the right answer over time. The question is what is "right" in each of those efforts, and the bar for what is deemed as "right" keeps getting raised or shifted.

Over the decades we have gone through every iteration of combining the three macronutrient groups (carbohydrates, fats, and proteins) to have better health and achieve weight loss. What you are told to eat one day quickly turns into what you are told not to eat another day. If you follow the trends, the heroes of nutrition at any given time quickly become the next villains. It is easy to become confused and overwhelmed. So, what does it mean to eat right? Just as importantly, who is best qualified to answer this question? Here's a hint: when you follow a plan to cut out an entire macronutrient group, you are no longer eating a balanced diet.

Any contemporary discussion of diet typically includes a discussion of nutritional supplements. There exists a big industry in vitamins and nutritional supplements. According to a study conducted by John Dunham and Associates funded by the Council for Responsible Nutrition,[1] the nutritional supplement business is a $120 billion industry. Vast volumes of research on the use and value of supplements are produced every year, not only on the value of individual supplements but also on the ratios of vitamin or supplements when taken together. For example, when taken in the right doses, Lysine and Vitamin D, are regarded by many as immune system boosters that could help in the prevention of illness, including the coronavirus. However, most physicians are reluctant to advocate the use of nutritional supplements, and few have been trained on supplements or the combinations and ratios of supplements to be taken.

Doctors are hardly even taught anything about nutrition, much less about nutritional supplements, in medical school. A study published by the NIH[2] found that only 32 medical schools in the United States out of the 106 who responded to the survey required a *single* separate nutrition class! Further, only 40 schools required the minimum education recommended by the National Academy of Sciences of 37–44 hours of dedicated instruction.[3] Put simply, fewer than 40% of the medical schools in the United States are meeting the *minimum* standard for nutrition education according to the National Academy of Sciences. Why then are we surprised that the number one health concern in the United States is obesity?

Sleep

Getting adequate sleep should be easy, right? Ha! Science shows that getting enough sleep is critical to myriad body functions, brain health, and even mental health. We need seven or more hours but getting comfortable for that long seems to be difficult for many. Advertisements abound for all manner of things to help us sleep. We have any number of mattresses, beds, covers, sheets, and pillows that promise to improve our sleep. There are CPAPs, mouthguards, and nose strips to help keep our partners form snoring. As far as educating doctors on the critical need for sleep, an NIH study[4] found this:

> Less than 2 hours of total teaching time is allocated to sleep and sleep disorders, on average, with 37 schools reporting no structured teaching time whatever in this area. Only 8% of medical students are trained in the use of sleep laboratory procedures, and 11% have participated in the clinical evaluation of sleep-disordered patients. Less than 5% of medical schools offer 4 or more hours of didactic teaching on sleep, most of which consists of 4th year elective experiences.

Exercise

Then we have exercise. Cardio was once all the rage. We forcefully took on a rowing machine or a stationary bicycle for an hour. Let's not forget the Stairmaster™ where we relentlessly climbed a moving staircase going nowhere. Then we needed less impact, so commercial and home gyms adopted "elliptical" trainers. Not long before the last payment was made on those, the industry uniformly seemed to determine that the new answer was anaerobic training. This came in the form of strength training. Simple weightlifting was replaced by "HIIT" or high intensity interval training. And so it goes—more confusion.

Every new exercise program includes a statement that you need to consult your physician before working out on an exercise machine or starting an exercise plan. So, it is reasonable to assume that doctors must learn all about exercise in medical school. If this is a disclaimer of liability on the part of the manufacturer, why recommend that you consult a doctor? If it is not a disclaimer, is it helpful? After all:

> The CDC reports that over 80% of American adults fail to meet the *Physical Activity Guidelines for Americans of 150 minutes of moderate aerobic activity per week or 75 minutes of vigorous activity per week*[5]. More concerning is the fact that this statistic has only improved by 4% in the past two decades. Conversely, when people do meet the recommended amounts of exercise, they benefit from a 40% reduction in all-cause mortality.[6]

Apparently, our optimism regarding the help we need from appropriately educated physicians is misguided. MDs, who by the way comprise almost 70% of all physicians in the United States, are licensed by the LCME or Liaison Committee for Medical Education. This group produces the standards for accreditation of medical schools[7] and is sponsored by the American Medical Association and the Association of American Medical Colleges. We will discuss this at length in chapter 7 on governance, but the short answer is that the majority of doctors graduate from accredited medical schools with little or no knowledge of nutrition, sleep, or exercise.

I signaled that "basic, clear, and direct" are important of effective teaching and learning. Here is a first attempt to distill some general ideas about living a healthful lifestyle,

1. Eat as many or fewer calories than you burn in a day.

2. Sleep seven or more hours a day.

3. Take a walk for an hour four times a week.

You are welcome to do more, but this is a darn good, straightforward approach for most adults. Unless you are trying to prepare yourself for the next Olympics or the NFL combine, this basic set of guidelines should contribute mightily to your basic health. Sure, you can focus on calorie composition, eat less, sleep in a sleeping bag or on a cot or in a hammock, and you can run a marathon every year (though at some point too much exercise has an injurious effect). But you don't need to do any of those things in order to have a baseline of health, and primary care is based on your individual baseline of health. "A health-care baseline is essentially where you are on the broad, complex spectrum of physical, mental, and emotional health," explains Mary James, MD, an internal medicine physician at Stanford. "This can be a critical starting point for achieving future health goals."[8]

TROUBLE

A friend, published author, medical doctor, and expert in primary care is Dr. Scott Conard. Dr. Conard wrote a book, *The Seven Numbers,* that has greatly influenced my thinking about an optimal approach to health in which he presents the keys to a comprehensive health focus through the acronym TROUBLE:

T is for training (or exercise).

R is for roundness (or Body Mass Index).

O is for oils (or cholesterol levels).

U is for unacceptable sugar (blood sugar regulation).

B is for blood pressure.

L is for lousy habits.

E is for exploding plaque in your arteries.

His point is well-founded, if you monitor and manage these key metrics, you will proactively manage your health. These metrics are the signs that show that you are most probably either healthy or that you are travelling down a path to or from poor health. To manage these metrics, you need to see your doctor no less frequently than annually and have regular blood tests to check the subset of these numbers that require blood testing, though most of the values do not require a blood test to manage.

These seven letters are intrinsically tied to eating right, sleeping right, and exercising.

Training can be as simple as a one-hour walk a day or, in today's parlance, 10,000 steps a day at least three to four days a week. Training helps all of your body's systems work better. You improve your cardiovascular capability, which translates into reduced heart rate, reduced blood pressure, weight maintenance or loss, and other benefits—most notably, virtually all exercise also helps improve sleep.

Roundness is a ratio of height and weight that can be determined by getting on a scale regularly. This is what we might call a lagging indicator because your weight is the result of diet, sleep, and exercise, good or bad, and it provides signals of things that you may need to change. Weight carried in the middle of the body can also indicate cortisol accumulation, which can lead to a greater likelihood of heart problems.

Oils or cholesterol (LDL and HDL) require a blood test to measure but reflect whether or not you are eating a good diet of fruits and vegetables, which no one argues with, and some form of protein, whether from meat, fish, or a powdered shake. We need oils for everything from our immune system to our cognitive capability. If we have too much of the wrong kind of oils (LDL), we may run the risk of heart disease and other health problems. If we do not have enough "good" cholesterol (HDL), we run the risk of diminished hormones and a diminished immune system, among other things. Having too much "bad" cholesterol can lead to clogged arteries and heart problems.

To determine if you have unacceptable sugars, again, you need a fasting blood test obtainable from your doctor or a testing organization like LabCorp, Quest or some other third-party provider with a prescription from you doctor. Again, the numbers included in this test will correlate to your diet.

Blood pressure tells you how hard your heart has to work to move blood through your body. If your blood pressure is high, that means your heart is having to work too hard, which may be a sign that something is wrong. High blood pressure puts a strain on not only the heart and on all of the blood vessels and organs. It could lead to weakening of arterial walls and produce an outcome that could include anything from heart failure due to a ruptured vessel or an aneurysm.

Lousy habits include things like smoking, not getting enough sleep, abuse of drugs, poor diet, and lack of exercise. Smoking is particularly and dangerously harmful as it not only damages the lungs but it also adversely affects the entire cardio-pulmonary system. For the last forty years, from about age five, I was on a mission to get my mother to stop smoking. Not only did I find the habit a health concern, I did not like being around it. My efforts were fruitless, and long after her plane crash I conceded that smoking was the least of her concerns, and if it brought her any measure of joy or respite from the pain, I should stop bothering her about it. Ultimately, however, lousy habits are frequent and sustained forms of behavior that, if not changed, can lead to illness or any number of bad healthcare outcomes. Lousy habits can also be the result of an addiction or they can lead to addiction, making the challenge all the more difficult to overcome.

The *E* in TROUBLE is exploding plaque, which is, again, linked to diet because it develops from having too much LDL or bad cholesterol in your blood system. The LDL forms plaque on the walls of your blood vessels, constricting blood flow and, thus placing a strain on your heart. Eating too much saturated fat lends to the creation of LDL and the corresponding problems with plaque.

What Is Primary Care?

Despite our best efforts, life and health do not always happen as planned or intended. Each of us will, at some point and for some period of time, get sick. Some of us will get sick often. Some will get sick for long periods of time. As we age, the probability of illness or debilitation increases, and the adverse consequences of illness or debilitation become more acute.

Let's consider the objective of healthcare. It should be, I believe, to maximize the quality of life for the entirety of our life. Because we are talking about the human body and the human brain, we are focused on not only the absence of illness but the presence of functionality.

This is where living changes from an individual sport to a team sport. We can do things to diminish the chances of becoming ill or breaking down, but we may need help in doing so. Rather than seeing the doctor when we are already ill or hurt, we can use primary care as a coach to help us maintain and improve our health, and then rely on that coach to heal us if necessary.

The first place to look for your coach is your primary care physician, though unless he or she has children, the term *coach* may be new. We hear the term "primary care" constantly but let's examine what services actually make up this term and what role primary care plays in your health.

While the term seems simple and straightforward, it is neither, and you are not alone in a lack of understanding. Many of us have no idea if we have a primary care physician or what his or her name is. Some of us can't define what a primary care physician does. Frustratingly, on the definition of primary care, there are many variations. The Johns Hopkins definition for primary care positions the primary care physician as one who provides an entry point to the healthcare system and who "coordinates and integrates care."[9] This makes the primary care physician more of a gatekeeper and referral source rather than an actual caregiver. It might be analogous to a prime contractor's role organizing all of the trades to build a house but not having direct responsibility for the delivery of anything in particular.

Alternatively, the American Academy of Family Physicians uses terms like "reliable first contact for health concerns."[10]

The United Health Foundation defines primary care physicians as those in the fields of "general practice, family practice, obstetrics and gynecology, pediatrics, geriatrics and internal medicine." There is no difference between "general practice" and "family practice." Further, "family medicine" is a combination of ob-gyn, pediatrics, and geriatrics. The troubling attribute of this definition is that is comes from a *payor*!

Lastly, primary care is defined by the Institute of Medicine (US) Committee on the Future of Primary Care this way:

> Primary care is the provision of *integrated, accessible health care services* by clinicians who are *accountable* for addressing a large *majority of personal health care needs*, developing a *sustained partnership* with *patients*, and practicing in the *context of family and community*.[11]

This expanded on a 1978 definition by the Institute of Medicine ("IOM") with emphasis on the patient, the community, and the notion of "integrated care."[12] The new additions changed the nature of the definition in scope and context, though not the scope of the healthcare needs of the individual. It defined primary care as "accessible." That is a relative term that we will discuss more fully later. This definition also includes the term "accountability" which is vague and unmeasured.

The goal of this discussion is not to fault any of the above definitions or to create a new definition. The goal is to understand what primary care doctors do.

Primary Care at Its Best

For our purposes, the 1996 IOM definition is most useful because it emphasizes important concepts, like the need for a "relationship" (albeit expressed as a "partnership") with patients. That immediately conjures the need for longitudinal data, both expressed as clinical data and anecdotal data. The IOM's definition also includes a reference to practicing in "the context of family and community." While this can also be criticized as vague, it nods to the idea of the social determinants of health, something that the industry has been discussing for years.

Necessarily, this means that the primary care physician is the first to evaluate, diagnose, prescribe, and develop a plan of treatment. It also means that the physician has a relationship with the patient, understands the healthcare implications of the family, and understands the healthcare implications of the patient on the community. Without going much further, I suggest that this definition would preclude most practitioners from characterizing themselves as primary care physicians and render them as disqualified from service in that role.

Additionally, we don't have enough of primary care doctors. Doctors retire. Doctors leave the practice of general or family or internal medicine. Doctors leave their PPO or HMO or lose their contract with the insurance company from or through which you get your benefits. Payment models and payment amounts change. Your doctor may now demand that you pay cash before your appointment rather than submitting the invoice to the insurance company for payment. You must pay for 100% of the visit rather than the co-pay only. Other doctors become concierge physicians, or they no longer take Medicaid patients or Medicare patients. The reasons for the undersupply of doctors vary from cultural to cost, from availability to accessibility.

One problem with the IOM's definition is that it makes it difficult to get good numbers on how many primary care physicians there are or how many there should be. The role as defined likely covers several specialties that are routinely being utilized as primary caregivers. However, the Health Resources and Services Administration estimates that the United States needs 6,900 more primary care physicians than we currently have to meet the current healthcare needs. Filling that need would go a long way to returning specialists to their intended purpose of care with a specific emphasis.[13] So, whatever they are, as stated, we need more of them.

Not far from the IOM definition, I propose that we use the following:

> Primary care physicians are those physicians with a direct and personal relationship with their patients. Primary care physicians are primarily responsible for the health and care of their patients using their longitudinal understanding of the patient, the patient's environment, and local resources available to solve the healthcare needs of their patients, including referring patients to specialists when needed, given the medical issue that needs to be addressed and factoring the advice of the specialists into the overall care plan for the patient.

What is interesting, though, is that medicine's recommendation is traditionally reactive rather than proactive. Rather than recommending semi-annual or quarterly visits, the recommendation is that a woman should see her gynecologist if she experiences "irregular periods or yeast infections."[14] A better model would be for men and, in addition to or in conjunction with their gynecological exams, women to see their doctors at least annually and get a set of screenings and tests that correlate to the key metrics of TROUBLE.

Beyond the Definition

The proposed definition includes important words and omits important words. The first of the included important words are "direct and personal relationship." A physician cannot care for a patient without knowing the patient. That does not mean that we must be best friends, but a reason that physicians have practices comprised of patients physically proximate to the doctor is that we need to know each other.

A patient's relationship with their primary physician in this context is mutual and bilateral. The patient must invest the time to go to the doctor, and the patient must share information with the doctor. Doing so creates an increased sense of connection with the physician and his or her office. It also provides the doctor with context for the patient and the patient's condition.

This is not enough, however. Analog information is necessary, too. Patients needs to share information about their families, the community in which we live, the amount and type of exercise we get, the supplements we take, the foods we eat, and other information to provide the doctor with that essential context.

For example, studies published by respected institutions such as the World Health Organization, the Kaiser Family Foundation, and many academic leaders in the United States and in Europe have for decades shown that a contributing factor to one's health or illness is the local environment in which we live. So, in addition to knowing the patient, the physician must understand the context of the patient's living situation. Someone who lives in an area with few parks or an area zoned as light commercial may have issues with air quality or have limited ability to exercise or even safely take a walk. Ideally, this information is either entered into an app by the patient or taken down by a nurse, which we will describe and discuss later in this book.

The next important words are "longitudinal understanding." The physician needs to know the patient over time, and the patient needs to stick with the same doctor to the extent possible. Even with good, portable records and familiarity, the patient/doctor relationship provides another layer of bilateral or mutual trust and insight. It is not reasonable that the patient should expect the physician to have instant recall on the entire medical history of every patient the physician's practice serves. Instead, the physician needs to be sufficiently familiar with each patient's major health milestones, good or bad, and, separately, be able to identify trends and patterns in the patient's health. Whether it is knowing about a surgery that happened several years ago or that the patient has suffered from consistent weight gain over the last two years, both are problems the physician needs to be able to identify and address.

Finally, note that the definition includes the word *solve*. The idea is that the primary care physician is not just a gatekeeper or a referral agent. There is a clear intention that this doctor is the one who is to provide the care needed. Having a primary care physician serve merely as a gatekeeper to other specialists adds cost to healthcare, is unsatisfying to both the physician and patient, and wastes precious time of both the physician and patient. Instead, we want as many issues as possible to be addressed and resolved, or better yet, prevented, by the primary care physician. Having one doctor who follows your care consistently over time can better equip your doctor to anticipate and address arising health problems. Prevention and early detection save everyone time, money, and distress. Placing the focus on your primary care physician to be a gatekeeper, as is promoted by the construct of most health insurance, shortchanges the consumer and keeps you from making vital contributions to your care without providing you the benefits of true partnership.

Specialists are not meant to be health partners. They are to be utilized to address specific problems rather than overall and ongoing health concerns. While expecting the primary care physician to solve most problems, we should not expect the primary care physician to be able to solve all problems. As a result, referrals should be made when appropriate. At the moment, referrals take place because the provider's system encourages or mandates the referral. It may also be the case that regulations encourage or mandate the referral. Whether a referral may or may not be the right answer depends on the unique situation of the patient.

To have an effective relationship, the patient must actually "see" the doctor, ideally in person but even a video conference is helpful. Of course, there is also the issue of individual choice. No matter what the definition of primary care is, the problem of seeing the doctor in a timely manner often starts with the patient's reluctance to see any doctor or caregiver, often dismissing going to the doctor with such declarations as "I am not going to the doctor!" "I feel fine." "It is just an allergy." "This will pass. I don't want to be a bother." Patients who have elected not to see a primary care doctor, who have not had screenings or tests that could identify health issues magnified by viruses and seasonal health flare ups, may also choose to ignore the symptoms. These patients may rationalize their choice. However, as we have now seen with the COVID-19 pandemic, a sneeze could be the sign of something significant, or worse it may transmit a virus or bacteria that ends up on a surface later touched or a hand later shaken. Concluding that any symptom is not something to bother a physician with can create a health risk. In this example, the risk is twofold—contagion and complication—both of which could lead to fatality.

I am not asserting that we must go to the doctor every time we sneeze, cough, or have a headache. It is neither appropriate nor responsible to go the doctor all the time; however, each of these symptoms means more when there is continuity in care, context with recent health trends and patterns, and an ongoing relationship with a physician who knows how your body operates. In each instance, the decision to seek care is, for adults, a judgment call of when to see the doctor made solely by the patient. For minors, it is the decision for the parent or guardian.

Do We Have Too Much or Too Little Healthcare?

When deciding whether to seek care, most patients tend to err on the side of less is better. This tendency is reflected both in supply of caregivers and demand from patients. To be clear, however, the biggest point to take away from this entire chapter is that it is a joint responsibility and a team effort to keep everyone healthy. That means patients need to go to the doctor, and doctors need to see each patient for sufficient time to understand the patient's needs.

Contemporary medicine has embraced the ethos of going to the doctor less, if not far less, rather than more. Over time, the use of primary care physicians has declined, and the supply of primary care physicians is insufficient. In other words, we appear not to be going in the right direction, as reflected by both supply and demand issues. Ultimately, the market will balance this out, but the behaviors of everyone in the market need to shift to reach the right balance.

The supply of primary care doctors is diminishing, and the ratio of primary care patients to doctors is increasing. Realistically, it is less lucrative and otherwise less appealing to become a primary care physician. In 2019, a record high number of primary care positions were offered and a record low percentage were filled.[15] Overall, only 41.4% of internal medicine positions in the United States in 2019 were filled by graduates of US medical schools—a declining trend for each of the last eight years—while the percentage of positions filled by foreign medical school graduates has increased and surpassed those from US schools. In fact, from 2002 to 2015,[16] the nation had a 2% decrease in the number of people with a primary care physician, and we may have 55,000 too few primary care physicians by 2032 according to the Association of American Medical Colleges. Even if no change were to occur in the use of primary care physicians, the Association of American Medical Colleges predicts a shortage of primary care physicians will continue for years to come when considering the combined effects of the rise of the millennials, who now outnumber all other generations, and the increasing death rates for the aging baby boomers with all of their correlated chronic and end of life health problems, and the increase in obesity of all age groups, starting in childhood.

This problem is more acute for people of color. Our healthcare system has structurally disadvantaged people of color, and physicians of color today make up only 4% of physicians. Why does this matter? A paper by the National Bureau of Economic Research found that black men treated by a black doctor are 49% more likely to get a diabetes screening, 71% more likely to get a cholesterol screening, and 56% more likely to get a flu shot. These screenings directly tie to the pre-existing conditions of those most likely to die from coronavirus. Too few primary care doctors of color exist in our healthcare system today. Too few clinics exist in our communities of color today. Both of these factors contribute to reduced access to physicians of color and this continues the problem of reduced usage of primary care physicians by people of color who are reluctant to be treated by white physicians.[17] The coronavirus pandemic has shown us that such undersupply leads to short-term illness and death and can lead to chronic issues that take more time to manifest but which could be either prevented or resolved early if diagnosed by a caregiver as a result of a regularly scheduled visit.

Who Is Using Primary Care, and How Are We Using It?

The short answer is that women use primary care more than men, children use it more than most adults, and the elderly consume a great deal of healthcare resources. However, for primary care, we have seen something of a decline. There are a number of factors driving reduced demand. The vast majority of us do not use primary care at all or do not use primary care in the right way. We have a culture that encourages a "toughing it out." This is particularly true with males, which means it influences boys and families. The patriarch of any family influences how the family spends money and the value placed on health. Boys want to please and emulate their fathers, so if the father dismisses care in favor of toughing it out or ignoring medical concerns altogether, the growing boy may be likely to do so as well.

The dynamic is different for men and women. Most women go from their pediatrician as their primary source of healthcare to their gynecologist. Pediatricians treat patients up to eighteen years old. The transitional point for women is often puberty, which leads women to see their gynecologist for the first time. The nature of that relationship between female patient and gynecologist is so personal that many women look to their gynecologist for regular check-ups, continuity of care, and for other primary care needs for their entire lives; however, that is a relationship issue and not a usage issue. Studies show that women see their doctors more regularly than men.

An NIH study found that:

> [T]he subsequent mean numbers of primary care visits and diagnostic services were significantly higher for women than for men. Primary care physicians may be more likely to order laboratory, radiologic, and other diagnostic tests for women who make more frequent visits and have continuing medical complaints. We did not, however, observe the higher referral rates to specialty care for men that others have found.[18]

The study found that women were more likely to use services, self-report worsening physical condition, improve better than men, and were more likely to use self-care and prevention than men. The study also found that physicians created different care plans for women as a result of the physicians' belief, influenced by their experience, that women had these attitudinal differences. A study published by the University of San Diego found that:

> Men were 2.7 times more likely than women to be influenced to seek health care by a member of the opposite sex (95% CI, 1.6 to 4.6). Married patients were 2.4 times more likely than unmarried patients to be influenced to seek health care by a member of the opposite sex (95% CI, 1.4 to 4.3).[19]

Our society also includes people with religious beliefs that discourage using physicians as contrary to their faith. Christian Scientists and Jehovah's Witnesses are two groups that fall into this category. Christian Scientists believe that prayer is the most effective healer. Jehovah's Witnesses go a step further and prohibit blood transfusions, even when required to save someone's life.[20] Unsurprisingly, these positions have been the subject of litigation and regulation, particularly when dealing with children's healthcare decisions.

One can also make the argument that differences in usage are based on socioeconomics and based on race. Both are true. Many who are poor have a difficult time either affording care or, as is often the case, getting to the doctor. While many of us take transportation and freedom of movement from one place to another for granted, the poor cannot. In rural areas, the distance to reach a doctor may be so great as to discourage use.

While every urban area is different, in many communities, the poor and less affluent must either walk or use public transportation. Where the distance is too great, they will either do nothing or take public transportation. Where they take public transportation, the choice will likely be one or more of the following: bus, light rail, or subway. The latter works to a large degree in urban, vertical cities. However, beyond New York City and Chicago, the choices are primarily light rail and bus. In either case, the time required to get from point A to point B can be significant. If the poor are working poor, this is doubly challenging. It decreases income and increases the cost to go to the doctor.

Again, the less affluent can do nothing or make the multimodal trek. There are two other choices in some communities. In Southern Dallas, many use a well-orchestrated group of church vans, or as my friend calls it, the "bulwark of the transportation system." This is a primary means of transportation for those seeking to get from to and from a doctor's visit, especially for the elderly poor. With so few choices, some, though not a significant percentage, simply dial 911 and travel by ambulance to obtain primary care in the emergency room. These are both less than optimal choices for many reasons.

Whether addressing the needs and options for care available to the young poor, the elderly poor, or the not poor, the conversation should revert to telemedicine. Think of how much time is wasted and expense incurred in physically going to the doctor's office. Much of what is addressed in these brief meetings could be addressed in a video conference call. It would save everyone a great deal of money if a patient could simply take a six-minute break and return to work after having seen the doctor by teleconference, fully equipped with a diagnosis or prescription or care plan.

Affordable video conferencing technology exists today, and the software is free. The hardware is not free; however, an app on a smartphone can support such a videoconference call. Other hardware solutions may cost $100 to $200 or more, including devices like Facebook's Portal, Amazon Echo Show, Google Nest Hub Max, and others. Teleconferencing is not a universal option; patients who are elderly, less technologically literate, or are burdened with physical or sensory challenges may need help, at least initially, learning how to use the technology, even though it has been greatly simplified in recent years.

Telemedicine has to peacefully co-exist with regulations, and we still have challenges with what I call government and commercial regulation. Governmental regulation limits access to care based on state licensing laws discussed earlier. This means that the doctor has to be licensed in the state where he or she is practicing medicine, which usually that means the state where the patient is located at the time of the "visit" with the doctor. While the current administration has put a moratorium on enforcement of the state licensing laws that would prohibit use of telemedicine, that moratorium is set to expire. At least one of the major insurance companies has already said that they are going to discontinue payment for telemedicine appointments the day that the moratorium expires, ostensibly because of fear of fraud and the inability to "measure." That this strains credulity matters not, apparently. That it would save time and a great deal of money to the patient and the provider is not subject to contest. State licensing laws, as will be discussed fully in a subsequent chapter, need to change.

Moving from access to affordability, remember that the doctor is compensated, by and large, for a six-minute visit, which may be a blend of access (six minutes is not much time) and affordability (if you are relying on insurance to pay for the visit, it can't go longer and still be covered). One should not have to navigate a bus, a train, and or a light rail system to get to the doctor's office, wait for a while, and then see a doctor for a time that may extend to or slightly beyond six minutes! Instead, I suggest that primary care physicians be allotted more time to spend with patients and be reimbursed more for those visits. Incentives should exist for both the patient and the caregiver.

The discussion above also assumes that there is a doctor willing to see you, who is affordable for you to see, and available for you to see. On the first point, doctors are decreasingly interested in seeing Medicaid patients because the reimbursement rate from Medicaid does not cover the costs of the patient visit. That reduction in supply of doctors produces fewer appointments available for Medicaid patients.

How Should We Use Primary Care?

The concept proposed in *The 60% Solution* for primary care centers on correcting three major areas of challenge:

1. Too few primary care physicians;

2. Too little research and training on basics (eating, sleeping, and exercising); and

3. The need to focus on and invest in creating health and prevention rather than spending dollars on treating disease after health has diminished.

First, we need to see primary care physicians who are educated and knowledgeable about nutrition (including vitamins and nutritional supplements), sleep, and exercise. Failing to get these basics right leads to a weakening of the patient's immune system.

Next, we need these doctors to be proportionate to the population, which means that if blacks comprise 13% of the population, then black physicians should comprise approximately 13% of the physicians. Further, that same proportionate composition must exist with primary care physicians even at the expense of specialists. As we have noted, studies[21] show that if the patient and physician are of the same sex, the doctor's recommendations will be different from those offered where the physician and patient are not of the same sex. Combining the findings of this study with the study on the effect of the race of the physician and patient, suggests that the composition of the physician population should somewhat mirror that of the general population or at least of the community served. If nothing else, patients should be made aware of the studies, the potential for inherent biases, and be provided choices.

Along with accessibility and training, it is clear, well-researched, well-documented, and unequivocal that effective primary care saves time, money, discomfort, and lives.

Early detection and prevention are a must. Early detection of a medical problem allows for corrective behavior, medical intervention, or other forms of care to be implemented to prevent the condition from worsening. Taking a blood test on a regular basis, for example, will allow the primary care physician to observe whether or not a patient's cholesterol levels are increasing and are in or moving towards a critical range. If so, improvements in diet and exercise can be recommended, and, if necessary, medication can be prescribed. This is a much better solution than discovering a patient has a heart condition following a cardiac arrest!

At least one estimate indicates that if everyone in the United States saw a primary care physician, the total cost of healthcare would decrease by $67 billion a year.[22] A separate study concluded that for every $1 spent on primary or preventive care, $13 would be saved.[23]

The irony here is that all of the signs are pointing in the same direction. Seeing a primary care physician regularly saves time, money, and lives. By getting checkups at least once a year, we can identify and prevent more significant (and costly) medical problems from manifesting. In addition, primary care physicians can better guide patients on the use of over-the-counter medications, preventive care options, and the lifestyle choices we are making. As a result, we will feel better more frequently and for longer than we might otherwise.

The alternative to effectively using primary care might be characterized as lazy, selfish, or destructive. The resources, whether in the form of human resources like doctors, or the capital-intensive resources, like hospitals, imaging systems, or urgent care facilities are all expensive. As we've already seen, we don't have enough of those resources for the model we are using today. This supply and demand imbalance drive costs up, and costs are going to continue going up until 2043 when the last of the baby boomers reaches their current age of life expectancy.

How Do I Pay for It? From One to Many . . .

Before we get to "how do I pay for it?" we need to know what "it" is along with the options for paying.

First, recall that when you get insurance from your employer, you are in a pool or collection of people insured. The insurance company evaluates the risk profile of that pool and then figures out what the cost to insure the pool is given its aggregate risk profile. At the beginning of this chapter, I mentioned that when you do things that improve your health, you are also helping others. You are helping family members and loved ones by not being someone who requires their worry and concern or time to care for you, but you also help everyone else in the pool of insureds by reducing the aggregate cost of care because you have maintained good health. Extending the consequences of your good health further, you are also helping your company with increased productivity and reduced absences. Still further, you are helping your community, state, and country by reducing the healthcare costs they will have to cover now or later in your life. So, when your health is good, everyone wins.

With the greater good in mind and now that you know how to use primary care and what to use primary care for, we can address the question, "How do I pay for it?" There are two options introduced here and developed later in this book.

Incremental gains are being made all over the country with primary care, but we have a long way to go. Primary care doctors are coalescing into large groups to gain negotiating leverage, and this is working. Now, some insurance carriers are allowing a form of primary care coverage to occur using a per patient payment per month coverage model. This model gives physicians more visibility and clarity around their cashflows, allows them to be more flexible with their time, participate in savings for the population of patients covered by the model, and reduces the time required by physicians to file claims associated with seeing their patients.

If we only did this portion of the 60% Solution, we would make great strides in improving the quality of health for all and reduce the costs of healthcare for everyone in the entire country.

Chapter Three
CLARIFY PRICING

S ure, there are instances when you don't know what the full cost of something is going to be under certain circumstances.

Consider this common domestic scenario:

My wife says, "Honey, I drove my car this morning, and it sounds funny."

"I will take a look at it," I say with responsibility and authority as if I am going to be able to diagnose the problem, as if I have the knowledge, time, tools, parts, and supplies to solve the problem, which also assumes that the sum of those costs is less than the value of my time (and my willingness to endure the fussing I get when, not if, I do not make the repair correctly).

I return, ask a series of questions designed as much for me to sound like I know what I am talking about as it is to diagnose the problem.

"I will take the car into the shop; be back in a little while." The door closes, and I am off to my local mechanic.

The mechanic needs more to go on than "it sounds funny." So, I leave the car with the mechanic, and Uber home.

In my example, my car is analogous to my health. I am not qualified to know what the problem is with either of them. I can only give a vague, nontechnical description of the problem, and I take it to someone whom I trust to fix the problem. I do not know what it will cost to fix the problem. In a rare instance, it is possible that the mechanic does not have the part in stock, does not know how to fix this particular problem, does not have the special tool or machine required to fix the problem, or does not have the training to solve the problem. If any of these shortcomings occur, I may need to take the car to the dealer, who will be more likely to solve the problem. If the problem involves work that the dealer does not do, the dealer may refer me to a specialist who focuses on solving the problem in question. An example of this might be body work because the car has hit something.

I also know the price of the components needed to fix the problem, because the parts have fixed prices that the mechanic or the dealer can tell me. I could look for competitors who may offer the parts at a discount on the web using my smartphone or a computer, or I can get the parts through this mechanic, who might be more expensive but offers me the convenience of not having to go to a parts store and the confidence of knowing that I have purchased the right part, and if there is a quantity or volume involved, like shock absorbers or oil, I can be certain that I got enough and not too much.

I can be also certain of the price per hour for the labor required to make the repair because that price is posted on the wall inside the repair shop, and I can look for competitors on the web using my smartphone or a computer. Again, I can have the problem repaired at a competitor's shop or I can take advantage of the convenience of not going to another shop where I do not trust the mechanic as much as I trust this one. The same is true if I need to take the car to the dealer or specialist. In each case I know the price of parts and labor before I authorize the repair.

The shop, the dealer, or the specialist will call me, and tell me what the problem is, how long it will take to repair the problem, and offer an estimate using the listed price of parts, labor, and supplies to fix the problem.

This is where the similarities to healthcare end, because there is a key element of difference. Whomever provides that price or estimate is responsible to the car owner to deliver the service at that price, collect payment for that service, pay for the parts, supplies, and all labor used in the delivery of that service and for the quality of that service. Note that if the shop or dealer or specialist does not pay the parts supplier or specific mechanic, neither can pursue collection from the owner of the car.

Healthcare does not conform to this model. Try telling the primary care physician that they are responsible for collection of payment from the insurance company and payment to all service providers in the delivery of that services. There is zero chance that will ever happen! If the patient goes in for surgery, who decides on the anesthesiologist? Not the patient. Who decides on the hospital? Not the patient. Who decides on the blood testing lab? Not the patient.

Healthcare Price vs. Estimate or . . . Neither

With a wry smile, I invite every reader to do the same with any provider of healthcare services. If you are ever bold enough to follow my earlier suggestion and ask your care provider what the price of the service needed is before you are seen by a physician or admitted to the hospital, you will find that any answer they choose to give will always be wrong. Yes, that is right: it will be wrong, not some of the time, not most of the time. It will always be wrong, unless you are offering to pay cash.

The questions that follow require a great deal of patience to wander through the maze that is insurance but let's start.

Is the problem you are trying to address covered at all by your insurance policy?

If so, is the service provider "in network" or "out of network"?

Are you asking what the total price of the service is or the price that you need to pay "out of pocket"?

Have you met your corresponding "in network" or "out of network" deductible?

Is there a "co-pay" obligation of the patient to pay a portion of the price even if the corresponding deductible has been met?

When it comes to an "in patient" or "outpatient" surgery or medical problem, the answer is that no one can know. Why? Because each of the providers involved in the delivery of service has their own price, their own relationship ("in network" compared to "out of network") with the insurance company and will, for the most part, bill separately.

What? Let's consider a common knee surgery. Involved in the procedure were a surgeon, an anesthesiologist, a distributor providing the prosthesis, a hospital or ambulatory surgical center, an imaging center (for X-rays and MRIs), a lab services provider (doing blood analysis), and a primary care physician (required to clear the patient prior to surgery). Each of these providers may be "in network" or "out-of-network," which means that the aggregate price of all of their service (the sum of all charges) will range from the low end of all providers being in network to the high end where all providers are out-of-network.

Is your head spinning like Linda Blair's in *The Exorcist*? Okay, let's go another step forward in trying to understand the question of pricing.

Networks Influence but Do Not Determine Price

The concept of networks may date all the way back to the 1930s. Who is to say? However, the concept of networks was given a steroid shot in 1973 when Nixon signed the HMO Act. This Act provided financial assistance in helping start "health maintenance organizations" or "HMOs." These organizations are networks of service providers who individually and collectively agree to provide services under the plan at a pre-determined or negotiated rate to those who subscribe, usually employers on behalf of their employees or individuals. Think of this as prepaid healthcare provided by doctors not selected by you.

That should sound problematic for all sorts of reasons. First and foremost, implicit in the structure is the notion of cost containment to the detriment of the patient and the benefit of the HMO. Second, the doctors selected for HMO are not selected by the patient and are participating at a discounted rate. The patient selects from the pool of providers selected by the HMO. In other words, the patient selects an option from a number of choices that has been procured by someone other than the patient. Third, the network is comprised of providers who are promised a greater volume of patients in return for a reduced price.

There are many other flaws in the model, but this overview provides a starting point for the discussion. What followed the development of the HMO was fear and loathing in healthcare! Employers were getting strong, negative feedback about HMOs. Nobody liked them because the conflicts above manifested in either lack of trust in the provider or lack of choice or poor quality of care or referral denials or all of the above. HMOs that were profitable, some asserted, were profitable because the capitation limitations imposed on care allowed costs to be contained to serve profitability. HMOs that were unprofitable were unsustainable.

So, the pendulum swung back the other way in favor of more choice, and by the end of the 1990s the model changed to permit more flexibility in a patient's choice of which doctor to see, pricing for services, referral routes, and other features. Nevertheless, the boost given to the HMO model by the 1973 Act caused aberrations and discontent in the healthcare industry for more than two decades.

While HMOs have lost favor, they remain today, as do their regulatory siblings like PPOs. However, we can derive important insights from this period in history that remain unchanged. The government as stakeholder will continue to attempt to regulate the market, seeking an answer based on the political will of the day. This was the case in the 1990s, the 2000s (with the ACA or Obamacare), and the election of President Trump, who promised to unwind the ACA. It is also true that insurance companies will continue to have networks where they manage their costs from the service providers using contracts with those providers comprising the network. And finally, the insurance companies will continue to penalize the patient (not the employer who pays the premium) by imposing co-pays, deductibles, and capitations when a patient sees an out-of-network provider rather than an "in network" provider.

Define "Price"

While we, meaning the stakeholders, proclaim that we want individuals to be financially capable, educated, and engaged in their healthcare, there are far too many barriers put in place for those three goals to come to be.

First, patients don't pay directly for their healthcare, and a provider's time with the patient is limited. The result is that the patient is not told what the price of the service is. Further, because the patient is not paying AND the provider has limited time with the patient, the provider is not willing or able to educate the patient.

Second, providers use forms required by regulators that are not negotiable and amount to contracts of adhesion: don't sign them and you are not seen by the provider. The forms don't make sense and are not subject to negotiation.

Third, lab reports and other reports are delivered littered with unintelligible acronyms making those reports unintelligible for the patient about whom they are reporting. They are designed for the doctor, not for the person ultimately paying for the report. This means that you not only have to pay for a report that you cannot read, but you have to pay someone to read AND interpret the report for you.

Stakeholders at every level of the healthcare experience have competing interests. The list goes on. Financially understanding is clearly not a goal. Education is not supported, and physician engagement is replaced with disillusionment for those who try and helplessness for those smart enough to recognize at the outset it is largely impossible.

The cold, hard reality is that informed people are not even able to use the same language and the same words in order to have a conversation about pricing. When asking what the price of a service, test, or procedure is, a consumer is asking for the sum of the prices charged for all of the services involved. An insured is asking what the sum of the "out of pocket" charges will be. The only similarity is the *perception* of price that the patient has to pay from their own pocket at the time of payment. Whether they are acting as a consumer or acting as an insured determines their understanding of price.

If the patient is insured, the answer to the question of price may relate to their deductible or co-pay. We generally assume that the insured does not care what the price of the procedure is going to be, that patients who are insured only care about what they have to pay "out of pocket." From the perspective of the insured patient, the amount quoted is not the price of the service; that is the patient's portion of the price for the service. It is an arbitrary number that is a function of the type of insurance policy the patient has purchased. It is not the price of the service. The "price" has no correlation to "cost" or to "value." Further, you cannot correlate the price of your deductible to anything involved in the service to be rendered. The patient's contractual deductible and co-pay have nothing to do with the time of the doctor, the cost of supplies (*e.g.,* gauze), or the cost of parts (*e.g.,* a pair of contacts or glasses or a prosthetic knee). The cost of supplies and the cost of parts, in this example, also cannot be priced.

The provider you ask about pricing will be befuddled by your even asking the question. They healthcare provider cannot answer and does not know how to answer or who to ask what the price of the parts is. The information is not on the web and cannot be accessed by a smartphone or a computer. The doctor or nurse cannot tell me in advance how long it will take to repair the problem or offer an estimate of my cost for that doctor to fix the problem. Because an insured patient's costs are determined by their insurance, their healthcare provider has no way of knowing what they might be.

Should you pursue the question of pricing with your provider or their practice, you will be fascinated or angered by responses, which will range from disdain ("Why do you care? Your insurance company is paying for it, so it is free to you.") to ignorance, with a hint of indifference ("I don't know, can you ask someone in billing?") to obfuscation ("It depends: have you paid your deductible? Do you have a co-pay? Who is your insurance carrier?").

The reality is that the answer any service provider should give is that "it depends." Actually, the answer is more nuanced. The price of care is different from how much the patient pays, though we tend to focus on the amount the patient has to pay. If we are truly interested in reducing the cost of healthcare, we must begin by asking the question, "What is the price?"

Cost vs. Price

Let's be clear. Price means the sum of all charges by all providers in the delivery of services to care for the patient given the diagnosis. Price includes the fees (or costs) charged by "in network" and "out of network" providers, even if they are determined using different schedules.

We cannot get to price without understanding costs; however, we also must recognize that hospitals should not be expected to price surgeries with precision any more than we should expect a mechanic to be able to price the complex superficial and mechanical repairs needed to fully restore a car after it has been in an accident. The reality is that there are too many things that can be uncovered or that become complicated or that are unanticipated prior to beginning the surgery. Hospital stays for medical issues, rather than surgical issues, are also complex. The point is not to understate that complexity, but rather to suggest that hospitals should have clear, published prices for the service components that go into the total bill for care. It is not difficult to price the medicines, the anesthesia, the hospital room with nursing and meals, etc. We can also price, either as a fee for service or based on time, any and all specialist services that would be needed. Each of these prices would include overhead and margin and could be applied as consumed. This cumulative pricing for complex services is not different than as is the case in any other industry.

Our current model of having insurance pay a percentage of gross billed charges for hospital stays is just nonsensical. It bears no correlation to anything as evidenced by this appalling metric: the hospital bills 3.5 times, or approximately 280%, of what it collects. To say that shortfall is because of uncompensated care is false. That is about 3%. Neither is it because of the insufficient pricing limits imposed on providers by Medicaid or Medicare, which would be like saying that because the group in front of you only paid for part of their meal, you must pay the rest. That would make no sense and is no more logical than charging a percentage of gross billed charges.

The State Government Is a Stakeholder, Too, but Not Terribly Concerned with Cost or Price

The problem of matching costs to price is not limited to the clinical side. Insurance pricing is subject to almost no consumer pressure at all. As we will establish in chapter 4, the reimbursement structure is not designed to encourage anyone to reduce the cost of healthcare. If we are going to have state regulation involved, then state regulators need to do the job properly. Most states don't in that they apply subjective standards, lax enforcement, poor reporting, and poor enforcement to the job. The Kaiser Family Foundation reports that "most states make little or no effort to make rate filings transparent and lack the capacity and resources to conduct an adequate review."[1]

Therein the matter of healthcare costs must include the government. Even if they are not the final payor, the government has rights and obligations that go along with the status of being a stakeholder. The government also has the right to pass legislation, create regulations, promulgate rules, handle administrative disputes, tax, audit, and police, but they seem to pay more attention to certain of these and less attention to others. The government also has the right, but not the obligation, to tax every transaction in the process, from the companies providing the benefit (a tax deduction) to the employee's receipt of the benefit (not taxed despite it being a form of compensation) to the caregiver's providing services which may be subject to sales tax, to the companies providing the services, which are subject to a "franchise tax" and an "income tax" just to name a few.

Where there are regulations, they usually arise out of problems identified somewhere in the system that need to be "fixed," and there is likely to be some form of civil or criminal penalty attached to violating those regulations. The government generally does a good job of identifying and prosecuting crimes arising out of misdeeds in the healthcare industry, but they can do better. Fraud and waste are abundant whether the government pays for the service or a commercial insurance company pays for the service. Indeed, the government collected over $20 Billion from fraud investigations over the last 10 years. Note that in addition to our research performed in 2016, the last five years have yielded the DOJ another $10 Billion in recovery.[2] Could they do better? Perhaps. Will they ever root out all fraud, waste, and abuse? Probably not.

Where they could do better is following up on rules they establish. For example, under Title 22 of the insurance code in Texas, insurance companies have three requirements related to the establishment of "networks" for the purpose of giving the benefit of in network status to providers. The three requirements include:

1. Give every one of the providers seeking in network status a fair chance to be in network.

2. Respond to proposals in a timely fashion.

3. Create a network comprised of a diversity of providers.

The Texas State Department of Insurance has the right and obligation to monitor insurance companies' performance on each of these requirements. For the purposes of this analysis, I submit we give insurance companies a pass on requirement number 1. It is difficult to find evidence and to prove that an insurance company did not give someone a fair chance, but the same evidence that would support a claim under either requirement number 2 or number 3 would likely also support a claim under number 1.

An example of evidence supporting number 1 and number 2 might be timeliness. As a general rule, one might expect an acknowledgement that an insurance company has received a proposal within thirty days of receipt. That is not a response, merely an acknowledgement. The response, one might assume, should occur in the following thirty days. After all, the proposal may be complex or require some level of sophisticated analysis, it could compete with other proposals, and there may be other matters that would delay a response. However, it is reasonable to expect an acknowledgement of receipt within thirty days of receipt and a response to the proposal within sixty days of receipt of the proposal.

The first barrier to accountability is that the proposal is not submitted to the Department of Insurance but only to the insurance company. That necessarily means that no one is keeping time while the process is unfolding, and any complaint will take a long time either through administrative process or litigation.

The second problem is the nature of the response. An insurance company can merely write a one-page letter and state that they decline the proposal. That may satisfy the letter of the regulations, but it will not satisfy the public policy behind the regulation that seeks to have a pool of geographically distributed providers comprised of a diversity of business models, operational capacities, and other attributes that inspires full and fair competition.

In the case of compliance with requirement number 3, the problem of failure to comply has even more dimensions. Whereas requirement number 2 addresses the problem of time and substance, number 3 is concerned with timeliness, substance, qualification, and other broad dimensions. so, the Department of Insurance has a reporting requirement for all insurance companies licensed in the state where the insurance company has to set forth where the "in network" providers are located and what differentiates that provider base from others. The reports have to be filed on a quarterly basis.

This is where things get tricky. Imagine that the insurance company sends in the report describing the composition of that insurance company's network. It has complied with the obligation to file the report. What does the Department of Insurance do? Well, theoretically, the report has a specific format with defined terms, is written in plain English, provides intelligible analysis, thoroughly describes all providers, provides a map of the geographic location and coverage for those providers, and includes other information that the department or the insurance company thinks is appropriate for consideration. Theoretically, the report is then reviewed and analyzed by the department, presumably by a capable staff that is of sufficient size to handle all of those reports filed. Subsequent to the review and analysis, someone from the department would either send a letter of satisfactory compliance with requirement number 3 above or send a list of things that were found to be either insufficient in the report or insufficient in the "network" requiring further attention and resolution by the insurance company.

This would be an appropriate time to point out that the Department of Insurance should not consider this to be just a competition issue or a just a fairness issue. The department should also be looking at cost because that will likely be an issue at the next rate discussion when it comes time for the insurance company to assert that their costs have increased thus requiring an increase in the premiums that can be charged.

However, there is another issue that creates a conflict for the department—taxes! That is right, taxes. Like many states, Texas has a sales tax of 8.25% that is applied to many of the goods and services involved here. Because the sales tax is a percentage, what happens when the price being taxed goes up? The tax revenue goes up! So, how does this conflict play out?

It doesn't! Why? Consider this scenario:

"Ash, this is Che'Nita from Acme Healthcare. I would like to get a copy of each of the quarterly reports submitted by the five largest healthcare insurance companies in Texas. Can you send those to me via email, or do I need to come by and pick up a hard copy?"

"Che'Nita, thanks for calling. No, we can't provide you with a copy of any of those reports."

"Really, why is that?"

"The reports can only be released subject to a Freedom of Information Act or FOIA request filed with the department. We will then process it and, if we can comply, we will let you know."

"You mean I have to engage a lawyer to file a FOIA request and then wait? How long will that take?"

"About two weeks from the date your FOIA request is approved, assuming it is."

"Okay, thanks."

"No problem."

Che'Nita calls the CEO and explains that to complete the analysis the CEO has requested, a lawyer will have to be hired, a FOIA request has to be filed, reviewed, and approved or denied, and then—if the FOIA request is approved and the reports are delivered—Ash can begin the analysis.

The CEO asks, "How long will that take?"

Che'Nita says, "They told me a couple of weeks from the date of the approval of the FOIA request."

"Dammit! I wanted this analysis prior to the next meeting of the Board of Directors so that I could make some recommendations. I guess I will have to push it out till next quarter. Go ahead with this. I still need your analysis."

Che'Nita hires an attorney, works with the attorney to get the request filed, and learns that the request has been approved. *"Good,"* Che'Nita thinks.

A few weeks later the reports are delivered via link to a cloud-based shared storage file system because they are too long to print and too big to email. Che'Nita downloads three of the reports, scrolls through the first, scrolls through the second, and then scrolls through the third. The process takes about a day and a half, in part because Che'Nita cannot understand the reports and has to spend time reading and re-reading each report until he's certain that the report is just not intelligible—at least to Che'Nita.

The next day, Che'Nita calls Ash.

"Ash, this is Che'Nita from Acme Healthcare."

"How are you, Che'Nita? Did you get your reports?"

"Yes, thank you. But I was really confused by them. Can you help me understand at least one of these reports or point me to someone who can?"

"Well, not really."

"Why is that?"

"We don't really understand the information that comes to us in those reports either. What's more, we don't have enough staff to set up a format or a template that the insurance companies can use to complete the reports and at least make them look the same."

"So, you are understaffed and the staff you have doesn't have the skills needed to do this kind of work? I am sorry, Ash. That must put you in an awkward position"

"I don't like disappointing people, and I like to be able to be responsive and solve problems for our constituents, but in this case, I just can't. The good news is that I don't get many calls like this. Not many people ask these kinds of questions or follow up. I don't know if that is because these issues do not affect many or if they are just resigned to the fact that they can't resolve the issues that do affect them. In either case, I am sorry I can't be more helpful."

"I appreciate your candor and empathize with your position in all of this. Thanks, Ash." Che'Nita, replies.

While these are fictional characters sharing a fictional dialogue, the substance of the conversation is almost a mirror of one I know of personally. I guess the good news is that we did not have to deal with the conflict inherent in the state sales tax issue. One can only imagine how the rate conversation must go!

The results of this multiplicity of conflicts among the stakeholders and the regulators of the healthcare industry are the absence of competition, the ineffectiveness of market forces, the absence of insight, the increase in bureaucracy, the increase of cost, the loss of time, and the waste of resources. This also leads to a decrease in confidence in competence of government oversight and effectiveness of government function.

Back to Price

The funny thing is that a price can quickly, if not immediately, be delivered if payment in full and in cash or credit card is offered at the time of service. Look at cosmetic surgery, which is generally assumed to include elective procedures not covered by insurance (bariatric surgery fell into this category for some time), or other treatments not covered by insurance (acupuncture falls into this category). In each case, a call or a web search or a visit to the practitioner's office leads to the answer immediately because the prices are listed or available from the person at the desk or answering the phone.

I submit that prices for all services should be listed so that patients can know what they are in advance. The insurance companies and the providers will assert that this leads to issues of confidentiality; however, every non-disclosure agreement and every confidentiality clause has an exception if the information requested must be made available by requirement of a governmental entity or request.

What is unique about the promise of cash? It is almost like the movie scene when the ET peers out of the closet extending its finger toward Elliott (Henry Thomas) just as Drew Barrymore is doing the same. A magical force lights up, and good things happen. When cash is on the table, we are overtaken with love and compassion and a different feeling washes over all parties involved to create a . . . *relationship!*

Publicly Post All Prices

The preamble to the obvious may have taken too long, but it was necessary to establish a foundation for this and future conversations—publicly post all prices.

Heresy, you say!

That is right, publicly post all prices so that all stakeholders can know what the price of all services to be rendered in the delivery of that care will be in advance of pursuing treatment. Public posting means that prices must be posted in all of the service provider's offices in a clearly visible fashion and on their website on either the homepage or a page that is dedicated to prices and is clearly identified in the navigation bar.

Posting all prices means that the price for cash, Medicaid, Medicare, and in network and out of network prices for all insurance carriers, public and private. This, again, is where the government cudgel is useful. The government can demand that anyone seeking payment or reimbursement from any governmental entity must post all prices.

Naysayers will immediately cry foul! Insurers will scream that this violates the confidentiality provisions of the agreements they have with the service providers. But this is not so! The government can mandate public posting with little concern for legal retribution from the providers, and almost all confidentiality agreements have exceptions for those instances where disclosure is required by law or by legal action.

In anticipation of the gaming most likely to occur, service providers must post this pricing in plain English and in a manner that includes all services to be delivered *by* that provider. One can imagine the service provider doing this with a list of ICD-10 codes or other billing codes and corresponding prices that would mean nothing to the patient. No, the prices must be posted with the same kind of clarity one might expect when they go to a spa. Moreover, the service descriptions must also include any additional anticipated services that will not be delivered by this service provider and must be delivered by a different service provider. (Of course, recommendations are appropriate.) Going in for surgery? Then the surgeon lists the services the surgeon is providing, and those other services required that the surgeon will not provide, like anesthesia, hospital, labs, images, etc. Should the surgeon be unwilling to provide an estimate for the total price (meaning the sum of all in network and out of network charges by all providers involved), then the patient should be equipped with the necessary information to gather that information themselves. If the market dictates the designation of additional providers is the choice of the providers, the market must also create a new position employed by the insurance company, the employer, or available as an independent service provider who will do that work and provide complete cost and pricing information to the patient.

The transparency created by public posting of prices will create a mad rush of activity that will reverberate throughout the industry. The initial reaction will be a cold rush of fury. Medicaid recipients will look disparagingly at the reimbursement given for their care and wonder if their health, pain, or suffering is really only worth a fraction of that provided under a private insurance plan for the same services with the same service providers. Comparisons will also highlight the effect on pricing when cash payments are compared so favorably with the private insurance payments. Insurance executives will fume that they are paying so much more while service providers will counter that the costs of processing paperwork and the administrative burdens demanded by the carriers, coupled with the negative cash flow from delays in payment, the legal risk of coding errors, and tort liability demand that prices be inflated to cover those costs and risks.

With pricing transparency, over time, likely a short time, prices will come down. Note that I do not necessarily believe that profitability will decrease. Market pressures will finally come into play forcing process improvement for administrative processes, technology adoption, technology standards adoption, improved security measures, improved electronic record retention approaches, portability of electronic records, along with many other changes. By way of quick example, the last fax machine exists in doctors' offices! After the initial round of shock and awe occurring from the tectonic shifts in these areas, costs and prices across the healthcare industry will begin to decrease to a commercial median and mean. Importantly, where price is outside the market norm, legitimate differences related to the delivery of the corresponding services by that provider will be understood by the patient prior to the delivery of those services.

To be fair, we cannot just look at selected elements of the cost structure and ignore others. We want equity, and we need to pay the near-term costs of the Solution and we must expect pricing to change slowly over time. The long-term costs will be more than adequately covered.

Modify the Tax Treatment of Benefits

I believe many of those commenting on healthcare issues today advocate "solutions" that are driven by ideological purity rather than economic viability. A Libertarian might advocate no involvement by government anywhere or at any time, which ignores the reality that some portion of our population will likely always be unable to afford care. A Socialist might advocate exclusively for a single-payor solution, though almost no country in the world may claim to have successfully implemented a true "single-payor" system.

While I advocate, unapologetically, for economic freedom, lower taxation, and, generally, less governmental intervention, I also recognize that our efforts to become "a more perfect union," also mean that there are some imperfections that remain in our union. Regulation and taxation address those imperfections.

Most of the 60% Solution is largely without controversy. How can folks really get to fired up about standardized accounting, standardized IT, reporting, or published pricing?

This next step is a completely different offense. I am certain we will have those who want to march in the streets on this. Both sides of the aisle in both houses will scream that the proposition I am about to unfold is everything from un-American to downright awful. To be clear, this will rankle many. It is perhaps the most unlikely of things to be considered an entitlement, yet it is. I am referring to the tax treatment of benefits. Specifically, tax benefits are a form of compensation. While they may not be taxed at the same rate or in the same way as all other forms of compensation are taxed. Under the present tax code, benefits are not taxed. We should correct this antiquated exception, and all benefits should be taxable to the recipient as cash compensation.

In what many might assert to be one of many relics of the legacy of Franklin Delano Roosevelt, we still live under the tax impacts of World War II. FDR knew that the production requirements needed to support the war effort would consume all available workers, and he was right. In 1942, the unemployment rate was 4.7% at a time when the labor participation rate was near 100%. The following year it was 1.9%, and in 1944 it was a remarkable 1.2%, at a time when virtually everyone was working. To appreciate how small this number was, remember that the labor force included everyone ten years old and older![3]

Those statistics mean that the labor market was a seller's market, and the competition for talent could be ruthless. FDR anticipated this, and capped compensation under the Stabilization Act of 1942. He then increased corporate taxes under the Revenue Act of 1942, raising them as high as 90% in some instances. Because the nation had a public policy interest in making certain that workers were healthy (aka "productive"), FDR changed the definition of "compensation." For tax purposes, FDR's definition did not include benefits as part of compensation. Instead, FDR created an exemption under the laws that allowed for healthcare insurance and other benefits to be characterized as a business expense while not having the recipient of those benefits be taxed on their receipt. Mind you, at that time in our history, the US population was far less than half of what it is today, about 135 million. In 1942 the United States was involved in World War II. Prior to the passage of the Stabilization Act and the Revenue Act of 1942, about 9 percent of Americans had health insurance or 12,150,000 people. Today, the US population is approximately 330,000,000, and approximately 10 percent of the population does *not* have insurance.)

In 1954, Congress enacted the Internal Revenue Act of 1954. It was the first major overhaul to the tax code since 1913. At the same time, the United States faced many of the same international threats it had faced periodically over the prior four decades. The geopolitical landscape remained fraught with risk of yet another world war. In 1954, the United States had just completed the Korean War, was financing the French in their war in Viet Nam, was anxious about the USSR, and increasingly involved in what came to be referred to as the "Cold War." Less than a decade after the end of WWII, we desperately needed healthy, productive workers and economic growth. While GDP growth was negative in 1954, it was over 7% in 1955.

Like the Revenue Act of 1942, the Internal Revenue Act of 1954 maintained FDR's flawed definition of compensation by continuing to permit businesses to deduct the expense of benefits and not taxing an employee's receipt of benefits as compensation. This treatment encouraged employers offering employees health insurance and other benefits in order to be competitive

Historically the Republicans tend to abhor taxes of any kind. What surprises many is that Democrats seem uninterested in fixing this historical anomaly despite their frequent assertion that taxation is generally good and necessary, though regressive taxation is bad because it disproportionately harms the individual the less money the individual earns. The fact is that the special tax treatment forgives more tax on the wealthy and forgives less tax on the working class and poor is just as regressive.

I believe that regressive tax policies are wrong, and that compensation should include salary, wages, bonuses, and benefits, so a key recommendation of the 60% Solution is to change the tax treatment of benefits and tax benefits in the same manner as income. The current tax treatment is wrong and regressive. It needs to be changed. To be transparent, my real hope would be that employers would "gross up" the compensation to cover the cost of the tax on benefits. This would not be an increase in real wages but would protect the purchasing power of the employee.

The current tax treatment does something worse by providing an enormous incentive to use health insurance as a lay-away plan for health rather than as a form of protection against financial calamity arising from a health problem. By creating a dependence on that health insurance at the lowest affordable premium, the present system of insurance incentivizes the market to embrace those plans that offer the lowest possible deductible, given the poor savings rates of Americans.

Further, this tax treatment encourages the disintermediation of the patient and the provider. The tax treatment robs the US Treasury of approximately $273 billion annually, and the tax treatment disenfranchises the individual employee and his or her entire family by eliminating their market power and eliminating their knowledge about the cost of services.[4] Most in the healthcare industry I have spoken to do not have any knowledge whatsoever about the points I have raised thus far. Their paychecks depend on it, yet they don't know about it or understand it. If they don't, how can anyone outside of the industry understand it?

The players in the healthcare industry have wittingly or unwittingly conspired to make buying healthcare services difficult to do and difficult to understand. It is a rarity in industry that buyers don't know the price of what they are buying, cannot control the costs associated with the purchase, and cannot negotiate the price with the seller. Though this is simple to change in concept, it may not be easy to do in practice.

Chapter Four
STANDARDIZE ACCOUNTING AND IT

I t may seem strange to link the professions and practices of accounting and information technology, but they are remarkably interdependent in most industries and this is even more so in the healthcare industry. Just keeping track of the codes included in ICD-10 requires a database and more compute capability than existed on the lunar module that landed on the moon.

First, let's start with accountants. As a profession, they are the ones least likely to excel at a dinner party! The website careeraddict.com voted accounting the fourth most boring profession,[1] behind "Security Guard," "Bank Branch Manager," and "Data Entry" but considered accounting to be five professions more boring than "Garbage Collection"! The good news is that, in the aggregate, they are "trusted." *Forbes* ranked accounting as the sixth most respected profession. (I note with interest that three of the top five most respected professions were in the healthcare industry: nurses, doctors, and pharmacists.)

So, the trusted, boring folks of the accounting profession are in charge of determining what the cost of healthcare is and how the cost is characterized. Accountants are governed by rules and guidelines, and they are trusted because not only do they usually know the rules and guidelines they usually follow them. However, in almost all cases judgment needs to be exercised in following the rules and, especially, when following the guidelines. When accountants consider issues like "allocation of cost," there is often plenty of room for flexibility in the placement of that cost. Guidelines require that the actual cost assigned should link to a "chargemaster" or "charge description master (CDM)," which integrates the costs into the amount billed to, and paid by, an insurance company or the patient. Ultimately, this should be considered "the price."

The rules and guidelines governing accountants have been developed to help businesses understand their costs, expenses, and profitability better, to help investors understand the performance of their companies, and to help taxing authorities make certain that when taxes are owed, they are paid. What happens when the rules and guidelines are not clear or when the rules allow the accounting professional to assign higher costs and the incentives encourage it?

First, folks will assign costs differently and the industry will handle pricing inconsistently. Second, the costs for healthcare services will be higher, because the incentives encourage it and the rules permit it. When price is determined using a formula that is based on an assigned "cost" plus a profit and those assigned costs are inflated, then profit is not correctly calculated, and payment is more than it should be. This is the case with healthcare. Accountants and executives are incented to inflate costs and the guidelines permit that inflation, so true cost and price are not known by the party responsible for paying or anyone else.

The government has a cudgel to wield here to compel change. While hospitals and other providers are required to comply with

Generally Accepted Accounting Practices "GAAP," 80% of the hospitals in the United States are non-profits. The other 20% are for-profit entities. Both rely on insurance companies to pay their bills, and it is fair to say that both also rely on payments from governmental programs. The latter is where the government can step in and demand that hospitals standardize their cost accounting by standardizing the chart of accounts and the corresponding chargemaster or they will not be paid.

Currently, hospitals create an invoice that enumerates the "gross billed charges." As we've noted, hospitals generally bill about 3.5 times, or 280%, what they collect.[2] Insurance companies do not pay a fee for service and so have no real interest in the amount of those charges. Because insurance companies pay a percentage of the "gross billed charges," and the percentage paid has remained fairly constant, insurance companies are, in essence, encouraging hospitals to inflate the gross billed charges as a means of increasing their return on their costs, thus inflating costs rather than providing any incentive or any reason to focus on reducing costs. This feeds back into the pricing of premiums, as the insurance companies go back to state insurance departments and complain that their costs have increased and therefore premiums must increase. This has created a perpetual cycle that we've been unable to break.

The influence of this problem extends all the way through to the compensation of the insurance company's CEO. A CEO is compensated with a base salary, bonus, and benefits, but their real money usually comes in the form of stock options (or their equivalent) that allow the CEO to benefit from the increase in the company's stock price that occurs during the CEO's tenure. The value of the stock is calculated by applying a "multiple" to earnings. If earnings on any given day of the CEO's tenure are $100 million and the multiple is 8, then value of the company is $800 million. That number is then divided by the number of outstanding shares to come up with a stock price per share. If the number of outstanding shares is 2 million, then the share price is $800 million divided by 2 million or $400 per share. If, on the last day of his tenure, the earnings are $150 million, the multiple is the same, and the number of outstanding shares is the same, the value of the stock has risen to $600 per share. The CEO has just made $200 times the number of options he received as part of his compensation package.

The key question becomes how can the CEO influence earnings? The CEO can use both operational improvements and permitted accounting rules, and the CEO is incented to do *both*.

Incentives Linked to Increased Cost: Dreams Do Come True!

Well, the price of the stock is based on the multiple of earnings an investor is willing to pay. So, if earnings go up from $1 million to $2 million, the CEO did not make $1 million. The CEO made the amount of the multiple times the difference of $1 million.

Right now, the multiple for UnitedHealth Group's stock ("UNH") is 18.59. So, if the multiple was the same when the stock was $1 million as it is when it is $2 million, then the CEO made $18.59 million. In reality, it is likely that the doubling of earnings would increase the multiple from 18.59 to more than 20. In this cost-plus model, accepting an increase of costs from the hospital of $10 million to $100 million increases the number of dollars (10% of $10 million changes to 10% of $100 million) that falls to the bottom line of the insurance company that increases the compensation of the CEO because earnings in this hypothetical went from $1 million to $10 million, which is then multiplied by the multiple of 18.59. So, the chain of events leads to a CEO's potential gain increasing to 18.59 times $90 million or $1.673 billion divided by the number of options held by the CEO.

Now, I am not suggesting that CEOs' follow this line of thinking consciously. It's more likely that the reality runs something like this. A pool of people is put together in a "risk pool." The risk pool is underwritten by actuaries who use statistical models and a number of inputs to calculate a probability that the insurance company will pay claims equal to a certain percentage of the amount collected in premiums. When that cost exceeds the cost in the prior year for a like risk pool, the insurance company asks for a rate increase. When the rate increase is approved, the expectation is that margin dollars will be greater than the year before. However, the job of the CEO is to work hard to make certain that the cost of the claims paid out is equal to or less than the cost of paying claims for the like risk pool in the prior year. If successful, the CEO's stock options are more valuable than described above! Worse yet, most senior executives in public companies have stock options as a component of their compensation package. The import of the inclusion is that each such executive has the same incentive: they are all in on the game!

The Impact of the Incentives of Increased Costs

Between 2008 and 2016 Medicare and Medicaid hospital expenses went up by approximately 4% per year. By contrast, hospital costs increased by 60% during that same period for private insurers, and insurance companies paid a fairly flat percentage of total costs. That means that insurance companies' costs increased. Keep in mind that hospital utilization is declining, and insurance company revenues are directly linked to insurance company costs. If costs go down, revenue goes down and profit goes down even if profit margins remain constant.[3]

Unsurprisingly, in our example UnitedHealth Group's (UNH) stock price went from $25.39 on March 31, 2008, to $266.04 on September 6, 2018, crushing the performance of all major indexes during the same period. Apparently, as hospital costs go up, so too do premiums and so too does the stock price for insurance companies.

Standardization of a chart of accounts is an accounting issue, and it is the first step in identifying the true costs of a hospital. Standardization allows for comparisons between providers and allows for similarities and differences to be highlighted. The costs do not have to be the same, but the buckets of cost need to be the same. Imagine if you have two hospitals and one has gross billed charges of $100 and the other has gross billed charges of $1,000 for the same service where one hospital is directly across the street from the other. Why is there a difference? Right now, there is no way to know, but if we had a standardized chart of accounts that forced hospital CFOs to bucket costs similarly, one could analyze the comparison and ask questions. Are they spending dramatically more on supplies at one hospital vs. another? If so, why? Does one hospital have dramatically more administrative expense than the other? If so, why? Are there elements that distinguish the nature or quality of one service over another? If so, what are they?

A standardized chart of accounts and chargemaster would allow comparisons between for-profit hospitals and non-profit hospitals, which is important because 80% of hospitals are non-profits. The running joke in the industry is that all hospitals make money, some just don't pay taxes. Consider the case of HCA Healthcare, a publicly traded for-profit hospital operating company—the largest of its kind in the United States. HCA's stock *outperformed* UnitedHealth Group's stock during the same 2008–2018 period. Creating a standard chart of accounts and chargemaster would allow truer comparison, improve costing and pricing, and improve competition, all of which leads to lower costs—actually lower cost for the industry.

Reporting Costs: And Then You Get Flowers

Standardized accounting is only useful if the accounting is made known to people who are going to do something with it. Incenting pricing structure changes is only useful if the data is there to support the change. After all, if the information is not communicated to the correct people, nothing can be done, if it's even possible to determine whether anything needs to be done at all.

Reporting should happen with a set of financials using the standard chart of accounts and chargemaster, but that alone is insufficient if you don't know what kind of work is being performed at the hospital, as some procedures generate more cost and more revenue than others. The composition of the procedures performed at a given hospital is called a case mix.

We found that a case mix report with a case mix index was helpful in determining both cost and price. These should be publicly available documents easily obtainable by all—after all, these hospitals are taking your tax dollars—and should be used for comparative purposes by everyone from equity analysts to the good folks in state insurance offices and the Federal Insurance Office. No one should have to go through a Freedom of Information Act request to get this information.

It is worth noting that this effort to achieve standardized comparable reporting will likely have several phases to it. As a first step, the governing departments and agencies will likely put out a suggestion for standardization that has a period of time during which the industry can provide the corresponding department with comments. This is the first instance where all hell will break loose, meaning that the lobbyists and trade associations will complain fervently that this is a horrible idea, their First Amendment rights are being trampled, and it will actually increase the costs of providing healthcare. Of course, none of this is true for this instance of government reporting over any other, but the complaints will still be lodged. Note that this too, meaning the lodging of complaints and the responding to complaints, drives up the cost of healthcare.

After those comments have been received and evaluated, a draft rule will be put out. There will be some period that allows for a migration from the current rule to compliance with whatever new rule or rule are finally imposed. Compliance will illuminate the shortcomings of the newly enacted rule(s), and at some point, the rule(s) will be modified. This is an iterative process until industry and government find a balance where all stakeholder interests are satisfied, or compromises are made, and the cost of compliance is deemed "acceptable" by all parties. Some will assert that the cost of compliance is such that large care providers benefit over small providers, but this is both not the case and also no more the case in this instance than in any other instance where compliance with government regulations is mandated (think Sarbanes-Oxley, Dodd-Frank, etc.).

While the issues raised above are accounting issues in nature, as you can see there is much more than keeping track of the numbers. The accounting rules are principles that include legal issues, tax issues, financial information, healthcare data, and how to keep track of the revenue, expense, assets, and liabilities of the service provider, be it a hospital or other clinical service provider. This information must be recorded and maintained somewhere. If we have abandoned pencil and paper, and I hope we have, the next stop on the standardization train is information technology.

Moving from the *What* of Accounting to the *How* of Information Technology (IT)

The next challenge needs to be the standardization of information technology. If you ever want to know how to make bad laws, give the power of the pen to a bunch of liberal arts majors who then become lawyers who write laws that require a thorough understanding of engineering, data science, cyber-security, and computer sciences. That would be bad enough, but to make it really bad, make certain that the median age of members of the House of Representatives is over fifty-seven years old and the median age of Senators is over sixty-one *et voila!*

This is relevant to our discussion because even if our representatives and senators had the prescience to study information technology in college, and the vast majority did not, they still would not have studied the technology available today because *it wasn't invented yet!*

Let me provide a little more context. The developments in computer science that led to the internet started in the 1960s as a way to transfer files between military and university research sites. It was largely unused by anyone else until the early 1990s when, after five years of trying, Tim Berners-Lee convinced CERN (the European Organization for Nuclear Research) to support a research project that ultimately produced what we now refer to as the worldwide web or the "web." The technological breakthrough allowed users to access websites and move from one place to another through a technology called HTML or hypertext markup language. The user could then read documents, watch videos, or listen to music, all through their computer.

While we hail the Industrial Revolution as a time of terrific and rapid innovation, it pales in comparison to what occurred in just the last fifteen years. During this era, technology and communications have changed dramatically. The iPhone was launched in 2007 and more than 1.2 billion have been sold since launch. Facebook went public in 2004 and now has over $55 billion in revenue, $22 billion in earnings, and 2.4 billion users. Google also went public in 2004 and last year had revenues of $136 billion and earnings of $31 billion. Amazon had revenue of ~$7 billion and recorded its first ever full year of profitability in 2003. Today, Amazon has revenue of $232 billion and net income of $5.1 billion. Instagram was launched in 2008, and now boasts over 1 billion users with 70 percent of those users under thirty-five years of age.

Meanwhile, we are only now starting to see the complexity of the challenges that those good liberal arts folks are equipped to address. Questions of public policy, ethics, morality, privacy, and intellectual property ownership are crystallizing into complex issues demanding attention. But, to add another dimension, this technology is indifferent and impervious to geopolitical boundaries. Privacy issues in Germany, for example, are dealt with differently than they are in the United States or India or even France. Also of concern are foreign-owned companies operating in the United States with alleged ties to foreign governments—like Tik Tok, Huawei, and ZTE—collecting personal data on thousands of Americans ostensibly for marketing but also for other reasons.

These rapid changes in technology require us to think about the changing nature of geopolitical boundaries. If you can use videoconferencing to support an interaction with a patient, why do state boundaries matter? As we've discussed, if the medical school is accredited by a national body, why do state licensing matters come into play?

Regulations Create Complexity, Risk, and Barriers to Entry

A quick review of significant legislation that affects the risk profile and the daily operations of all healthcare facilities are HIPAA, or the Health Insurance Portability and Accountability Act, passed in 1996; and HITECH, or the Health Information Technology for Economic and Clinical Health Act, passed in 2009.

HIPAA sought to make certain that individuals could retain their health insurance if they moved from one employer to another or if, for any reason, the individual stopped working. HIPAA also directed the Department of Health and Human Services ("HHS") to create rules governing the protection of patient information and standards regarding the electronic transmission of patient information.[4] Virtually every piece of documentation shared by or about the patient is covered by HIPAA. HHS would take more than ten years to get standards in place related to the electronic transmission of that information, and they have been updated periodically ever since.

The HITECH Act was created to encourage use of electronic health records "EHR" throughout the healthcare industry. It also created a set of incentives and penalties related to compliance with the obligations set forth under the Act. Less clear, however, was what an EHR was and how it differed from another poorly defined term: the electronic medical record or EMR. Deviating from alliteration, the personal health record or PHR is also included in the terms to be explained.

A way to think about this is to define an EMR as a medical record developed by a care provider that relates to a particular facet of service, such as a lab report or the physician's notes from an office visit. An EHR would be the information related to a health problem, like a blood test for sickle cell anemia or the sum of all EMRs and visits to clinics over the life of the patient. So, an EHR might include several EMRs. The Patient Health Record or PHR is just another term for EHR, and is, similarly, the full, collected, and developed record that should be owned and maintained by the patient.

EHRs, EMRs, and PHRs are distinctive types of files, but many in the industry use them interchangeably or in a way contrary to the definitions above. Just to be clear, the standards for all of these records should be the same and consistent, and the records themselves should be written in "plain English" and intelligible to the average American.

HIPAA defined what information included in these records should be protected, defined the entities subject to the regulation responsible for protecting the information, and established standards for transmitting the record. The HITECH Act encouraged use of electronic records. But neither piece of legislation really defined any standards that addressed the real problems of maintaining these records. In this regulatory vacuum, the "globalists" went to work again and adopted "Health Level 7" or HL7 likely because, in part, HL7 had been adopted by more than thirty-five countries other than the United States.[5]

The work on standards is maddening, and even its description is maddening. If one develops software it must comply with a maze of standards. In addition to working, the software must be "certified" by an "Authorized Certification Body" that has been approved by the Office of the National Coordinator for Healthcare Information Technology "ONC-ACB"). Of course it does!

You cannot make this up!

Let's try to follow the trail. The Secretary of HHS has someone responsible for coordinating healthcare information technology. Well, "responsible" may be a little strong. The "Coordinator" selects the certifiers. As of this writing, this person is Donald Rucker, and his title is "Coordinator." So, when he goes home at night and his spouse asks what he did all day, his response is "I coordinated." Mr. Rucker's office approves folks who want to do the work of "certifying" EHR and other forms of software that can be used in healthcare. The folks doing the certifying are either an organization or a group of organizations that have been authorized by the Coordinator.

Failing to do things according to the rules brings about great risk for all involved. If the ONC-ACB wrongly certifies an application, the developer is liable. If an application is sold or licensed that does not comply with the standards or a healthcare service provider uses software that does not comply, the offending party may be subject to civil and criminal prosecution, fines, and even jail time. It gets worse! In addition to all of the other certifications and approvals, if you want to use that EHR in conjunction with Medicaid or Medicare in any way, there is an additional approval required from Centers for Medicare and Medicaid Services ("CMS")!

Substantial and frequent reference throughout the regulations is made to "interoperability" of the software and the data. Implicit in this notion is that if the application in question is "interoperable" then the data or the application is "portable." This is not necessarily the case.

The issue is not that the technology does not work, but rather that the technology does not allow the portability of files and records desired. Currently, electronic health records are not portable. The patient does not own the data. The patient does not have access to the information necessary to determine if one application from one healthcare system works with other departments in that same system (sad, but true) or if it will work with other systems. Further, the patient has no bargaining power to compel use of the application being used by the patient.

Think of it this way. You likely have your driver's license in your wallet. Huge amounts of data could easily fit on a similarly sized card. Alternatively, like most debit cards, a chip on a card could be used to authenticate a user's access to medical data and other personal health information related to that person, which could be stored in the cloud or on a company's server. Why has this not been done? Because all providers are discouraged from doing so as that would make it easier for the patient to shop for services and to leave one doctor or hospital or insurance carrier and go to another. This is true of the patient's EMR and the EHR.

Even where electronic recordkeeping currently exists and is meant to work, it doesn't work. Recently, my primary care provider sent a text message to my smartphone notifying me that I needed to confirm my appointment and check in for that appointment. The "appointment" was to be a phone call to follow up on blood test results. The phone call made it more convenient for me and for my physician. I was eager to hear the results and getting them was time sensitive as they had to be sent to my orthopedic surgeon that day. I was having my knee replaced that very week.

The text provided me with a link to a "patient portal" that allowed me to set up an account. The portal would contain all my personal health information provide an encrypted communication platform over which the doctor and nurses could communicate with me on issues related to my health. This expensive set of steps supported by software, expensive to my doctor, added *zero* value to the interaction, the relationship, or the healthcare outcome.

So, I linked to the portal and signed in. Oddly, the patient portal was branded Athena Health with whom I had no relationship whatsoever. Athena was and is not my insurance company, nor has it ever been. I did not ask for Athena's mobile application, much less pay for it. Only because I knew that my physician had used it before did I continue to the next step: patient check in. All together now, say: "HIPAA Issue"!

The app then asked me to "check in" for my appointment. The button looked much like the one used in getting your boarding pass for a flight. So, I clicked on a bar, and it sent me to a "payments page" saying that I had a co-pay for my visit. I knew that I did not have a co-pay for my visit but figured that I would enter my information so that I could pay for things, if needed, through this portal. That would make things easier for me and for my physician in the future.

I entered my name, credit card number, email address, and cell phone. Then, there was a field for my billing address. I entered the billing address and looked longingly at the "Continue" button thinking that with one press I would have reached the promised land of check in!

But . . . it was not to be.

The app told me that there was an error in processing my credit card. Knowing that my account was in good standing and my issuer was still standing (you never know these days), I double-checked the application.

It turned out that the credit card was not really the issue. I noticed that there was a lag in the application's response to my pressing the "Continue" button during which time the application truncated the field for my street address thus leaving the field with an address that could not be recognized by the credit card company. That's right, the field was too short! No, my address is not some form of multi-syllabic name from a different language that included too few vowels. The address was 25 Scottish Vista Park—plenty of consonants, plenty of vowels, and an actual address used many times with dozens of other online transactions.

Undeterred, I backed out of the payment page and closed the application. The application then confirmed my check in with a text message (what happened with my "encrypted communications platform"?) stating that I should arrive fifteen minutes early for my visit with the doctor. What?

This was an appointment for a phone call to take place at 8:30 A.M. on Monday for which there was no co-pay. Instead of simply sending me a text message through the same un-encrypted communications platform that had been used on countless occasions before, I was taken on a long goose chase riddled with errors that did not provide *any* additional content, value, or sense of well-being. The entire experience with the portal created additional work and likely violated, technically, a number of laws, because I had no contractual relationship with this provider. After all of this, I sent a text to my doctor and his nurse, as I had done so many times before, confirming my 8:30 A.M. phone call with the doctor to review lab test results.

Concerned for the doctor and his clinic, I thought I would give his COO a call just to let her know of my experience. She has not yet called back. Several weeks, the phone call, held at the correct time, and my knee surgery have now passed. When I brought it up with the physician, he was dismissive stating "oh, that is just a generic text message sent by the application" and did not address any of the other issues with which I dealt or the concomitant frustration arising out of those issues. Not only was he unconcerned with the issues, he was unconcerned with fixing the problem.

Compliant and Unintelligible

The good news is that the lab results were posted in the portal, and I could see them once I'd gone through the right pages to get there. The bad news was that the lab results are unintelligible to all but those trained to read the reports.

What does this mean?

Report	Result	Ref. Range	Units	Status	Lab
TSH	1.780	0.450-4.500	ulU/mL		

From this, I can discern nothing. (Not to worry though, because this is a certified EMR!) This lab report provides *zero* value to the patient for whom it is intended. I do not know if the test indicates that there is a problem. If there is a problem, what can I do about it? How long will it take to fix it? If it is not a problem, as appears to be the case given that I am within the "Ref. Range," what was being tested? Remember, this is information provided in the portal the patient is supposed to access to learn about his or her own condition. The only thing I learned is that I need a doctor to translate these acronyms into something intelligible and make the information actionable.

Then, There Is the Legal Question . . .

This begs another question. As I meandered through the portal application, I notice that many of the areas that include patient information (my patient information) have incomplete or no longer correct information. Can I fix that in the application? If I do fix the patient information in the application, does my physician or nurse have some sort of notification that lets them know I have changed it so that they are updated with my patient history? Does it change the legal liability if I change the patient history rather than ask them to change the history? Etc., etc., etc.

More importantly, if I discontinued my relationship with my doctor, I would not have access to that portal as my login and password would be disconnected. I have no idea how I would take that electronic medical record with me to a new service provider. Sure, my doctor has an obligation to give me a printed copy of my record and he must maintain my record, depending on the state in which he is practicing, for seven years from the last date of service.

That means that someone must manually enter that information into a new electronic record. Who does that? How quickly will they do it? Who pays for that? Who is responsible for errors in the transcription?

Further, what happened to all of the information collected by the knee surgeon who performed the knee replacement later that week. That information never gets fed into my "EHR" maintained by my primary care physician, but it is critical information for my primary care physician. The same problem exists when any patient meets with any other caregiver. While I emphasized in chapter 2 how critical primary care physicians are, primary care physicians are wholly unprepared for the responsibility they desperately want and patients desperately want them to have. Given their existing patient loads, most doctors do not have the capacity or the technology to ingest patients easily or seamlessly, and many do not have the education needed to treat all of the concerns.

Leaving one provider for another and having patient data ported from one provider to another is not easy. Both require common IT standards and protocols. McKesson's application, a software and services provider, does not easily translate to Cerner's, a software and services provider, which does not easily translate to Epic's, another software and services provider, just to name a few.

The problem exists every day for patients when physician practices, hospital systems, and other clinical service providers are financially healthy. However, this leads to material financial, legal, and health issues when hospitals or physician practices are financially unhealthy, are purchased, or close. Migration from one system provider to another may take more than a year. That is both costly and problematic for all of the stakeholders involved. In light of this, consulting firms, collections firms, "revenue cycle management" firms, and other organizations have created a business model out of this furball of regulations.

The Dire Consequences of Compliance

Perhaps worse than medical records being unreadable are the many unintended consequences of compliance. Doctors, nurses, and other clinicians report that they spend too little time making eye contact with patients. They also feel as though they are spending less time speaking with patients, both of which are consequences of looking at tablet or a computer screen to ask prescribed questions and complete online forms in an application they are required to use. Clinicians complain about feeling more stress than ever. "Burnout" is increasingly a problem for many care providers, and suicide rates for physicians have skyrocketed in recent years. How does one reconcile the current information gathering process with the sentiment in this quote: "The best way to care for the patient is to care for the patient"?

A Better Way

It should come as no surprise to the reader that I believe the answer lies in market dynamics. While a product or service is developed out of someone's observation of a need in the marketplace, the product or service is developed over time based on market inputs. What does work and what does not work? What can we afford or not afford to include in the offering? How are customers using the product or service? What are their complaints or concerns? And so, on it goes. Failing to address those questions in a way that leads to broader customer satisfaction and market adoption leads to market failure and the end of that product or service.

Digging another layer into the dynamic, the marketplace does not prescribe the features, functions, benefits, or constraints under which the product is used or delivered. Instead, each new product or service either starts from a completely new perspective on a addressing a known problem or is as an incremental advancement of an existing product or service and marketed as a different approach to addressing a known problem. The process of development in healthcare products or services is the same, but it includes disproportionate levels of input from governmental regulations, which are oftentimes inconsistent with one another and often stunt or altogether prevent development.

Reading through the articles that consider the basis for legislation and regulation and even the regulations themselves, one can see the struggle between competing approaches to common problems become manifest. There is a regulatory rally cry for "interoperability," and then the struggles begin in earnest.

Consider this from a genuinely thoughtful and academic paper published in the *Journal of the American Medical Informatics Association* (JAMIA), written by Jeffrey M. Ferranti, MD, R. Clayton Musser, MD, MS, Kensaku Kawamoto, and W. Ed Hammond, PhD, and titled, *"The Clinical Document Architecture and the Continuity of Care Record: A Critical Analysis"*

> This paper addresses one component of that set of standards: the ability to create a document that supports the exchange of structured data components. Unfortunately, two different standards development organizations have produced similar standards for that purpose based on different information models: Health Level 7 (HL7)'s Clinical Document Architecture (CDA) and The American Society for Testing and Materials (ASTM International) Continuity of Care Record (CCR).

The irony here is that this ecosystem that is largely born out of regulations is returning to commercial market standards. We have two acronyms. that signal reversion to the commercial mean. The first, is CDA, or Clinical Document Architecture, which stores and moves data from one healthcare system to another. The problem is that the data is just that, data. It is not communicated in a way such that the data is put in the "right" place in the patient record. In other words, while the data is communicated, it is not done so in a way that is usable or useful to clinicians.

The second acronym is CCR, or Continuity of Care Record, which applies its own structure for the data communicated by the CDA. In other words, while the CDA may convey 2000 Main Street, the CCR would identify this as the street address of the home of the patient.

Both the CDA and CCR use XML, a protocol used throughout most industries and not unique to healthcare. The CCR XML was developed by a standards organization without an economic interest in the code and is free to users. This leads to adoption by more developers and greater "stress testing" across different use cases.

Note, however, that none of this addresses the clinical needs of the patient! Society broadly, but clinicians, employers, insurers, and even family members specifically, complain about the need for greater engagement with one's own health and healthcare. But no aspect of this passive recordkeeping model is patient-centric.

If the design of the recordkeeping system were patient-centric, the system would function more like this: the patient would get a notice via encrypted email or text message from the physician's office telling the patient to get a blood test; the patient would stop at the drugstore or grocery store to get a disposable device that draws blood with a tiny pin prick to the finger; the blood sample would be analyzed by the patient's smartphone, and the results would be posted in an app that was designed for use by patients and written in plain English. The report would compare the elements of the blood test to normal ranges and would also be informed by the patient's entire medical history. Artificial intelligence built into the application, would anonymously run the results through databases (think Watson) that have ingested all of the medical history on all of the healthcare issues the patient has or has had coupled with any symptoms currently presented by the patient. Recommendations would be posted in the patient application for review by the physician. The physician and patient would then have a videoconference call to discuss the results and next steps.

In this example, the patient is a subscriber to the application, owns the data, and has allowed access to a care provider the patient deems appropriate. The patient understands the analysis, understands the recommendations, and can easily seek multiple or alternative recommendations based on their actual data through the healthcare provider of their choosing.

Note that the key issue here is that the industry lost the notion of patient as the "customer" in its approach to designing the recordkeeping system. Instead, the "customer" may be physician, the insurance company, the employer, or any of a number of others in the ecosystem. The easy way to identify the customer is to identify who is paying the bills, and that is the problem because the payor is not the customer here and that disconnection creates a domino effect of problems, partial solutions, regulations, workarounds, and distress.

Chapter Five
MODIFY HSAs

W hat if you could get healthcare for less?
What if you could comparison shop for direct healthcare expense?

What if you could pay for healthcare yourself?

These are not silly questions. They are not rooted in unreasonable demands, and the goal implicit in each should be achievable.

My wife often says that a mother is only as happy as her saddest child. As a nation, we should all be weeping, because so many of our people are suffering. Whether illness or injury, pain and discomfort are things we should endeavor to fix as quickly as possible and to do our best to avoid altogether.

Earlier, we discussed the need for pricing transparency. Here, we examine how to reduce costs by leveraging the buying power of the patient. In other markets this might be called the power of the consumer. The difference is that in those other markets, the consumer is the one who directly pays the bill. In the healthcare industry, the consumer seldom pays the bill. insurance companies or the government typically pay the bill, and this is precisely at the heart of the problem.

You'll recall that prior to 1944, fewer than 10 percent of the US population had health insurance. Then, most Americans paid for their healthcare directly. However, when Franklin Delano Roosevelt made health benefits an allowable expense not taxed as income by the federal government under the Revenue Stabilization Act, it increasingly progressed to insurance paying the bills of patients rather than patients paying the healthcare provider directly, whether it be a doctor, a hospital and even the packaged service provider . . . the pharmaceutical company.

With one company between the patient and the provider, things could be slightly complicated, even dysfunctional. Our present reality is far worse. The employee gets the insurance from their employer, who gets it from the broker, who gets it from the carrier, who has the insurance premium approved by the state in advance or, in some states, in arrears.

Most of us would agree that our insurance system is a jumbled mess of both federal and state laws, so the impact in each state varies. Despite being something of a healthcare insider, my curiosity has turned to incredulity which has turned to frustration which has, on occasion, turned into outright anger at those legislators and regulators who have allowed this system to develop. I hear others who know far less about the actual systems at work experience similar emotions just trying to get a medical bill paid.

More frightening than the consumer's surrender of agency in managing their own care is the popular notion that healthcare is a right and that it should be free or should be provided for by a single payor. In no instance has that worked. Despite what you might have read, Canadians who have a single payor system often come to the United States and pay personally for many healthcare services to avoid lengthy wait times. In fact, the Fraser Institute's 2015 report stated that the number of Canadians seeking treatment in the United States had jumped over 25% from the previous year.[1] Of course, we have long since decided that having a company that is a monopoly in an industry or a market is bad—see the Sherman Antitrust Act, for example— but many advocates ignore that and prefer to make healthcare a state-sponsored monopoly. Perhaps the same advocates have concluded that the Veterans Administration has done such a fine job serving nine million current and former members of the military that it should now be a model for providing care to over three hundred and thirty million Americans! Sarcasm noted and intended!

If single payor is not good and private insurance is not good, what then is the solution? Given that The 60% Solution is not doing away with government payment in the form of Medicaid or Medicare and given that The 60% Solution is not advocat- ing an elimination of private insurance, the answer is clearly a blended approach where accountability and market forces are at work for the entirety of the market.

Empower Patients to Pay Directly

Central to The 60% Solution is the need for direct payment as frequently as possible and for the patients to know their doctors and nurses. Beyond their caregiver, we also need patients to pay directly for lab tests, X-rays, and MRIs.

Throughout I have emphasized the need to have a direct relationship with care providers. We need patients to know their doctors and nurses. We also need patients to pay their doctors. Patients need to have a direct relationship with their caregivers, not simply pay incrementally now for the assurance of service in the future for which they will seek reimbursement or for which a doctor will process a claim that will be contested and paid (or not paid) even further into the future. And if the healthcare provider is not paid, they must send endless collections notices and finally a collections team after the patient.

Today, we pay for insurance we hope not to use. If we do need to use it, we seek reimbursement, or the doctor or caregiver seeks a reimbursement. We usually don't know the doctor or caregiver and we do not have a clue as to what the price is for any service needed. Currently, that reimbursement may come much later or not at all, and we have no idea why it has been delayed or not paid. My next assertion was to start, "the worst part is," but it is really hard to pin down what the worst part of this is. So, let's just catalogue the bad that comes out of this remarkably illogical model of payment.

If you have a medical problem requiring a visit with a doctor, you are likely there because you're not quite sure what you need but you trust that the doctor will know what to do. You go to a doctor who has completed undergraduate school, medical school, and may have been educated beyond that with internships, residencies, and/or additional training, and certifications. As the patient, you assume that the person with whom you are dealing is interested in your problem being solved. Consistent with that assumption is the fact that that there are shared moral, ethical, and economic interests that collectively should encourage the care provider to give the patient what the patient needs.

There is an imbalance of knowledge between the care provider and the patient. The same imbalance exists with a lawyer, an accountant, or any other professional. In fact, it exists anytime you are paying someone else for a service where you don't have the knowledge or experience to take care of yourself. I've already suggested the analogy of the auto mechanic. Cars have become such complex systems that the people who repair them are increasingly specialized, trained, and have an abundance of advanced expensive technology to diagnose and fix problems.

Let's assume for the moment you have a problem with a car—the low tire pressure light is on indicating that there is a problem with a tire. You take the car to the garage and are told that there is a puncture in the tire. You're told by the mechanic that you need a new tire.

"What will that cost?" you ask.

"Two hundred fifty dollars, plus taxes and fees" the mechanic says.

"Is there another solution?"

"A patch."

"Can you patch the tire?"

"Yes, but I can't guarantee how long the patch will hold."

"How much will the patch cost?"

"$25, but, again, I can't be certain how long the patch will last. You will probably be fine for a few thousand miles."

Through the course of this exchange both parties have learned more about the problem, the alternative solutions, the costs, the risks, and consider the alternatives in light of your ability to pay before deciding on a course of action. In the healthcare analog, you don't know what the cause of the problem is or what the solution is when you go to the doctor. However, it becomes worse because you also don't know and have no way of finding out what the price for the service is.

The patient has insurance that has a co-pay obligation and an annual deductible. Additionally, the amounts to be paid to the doctor are linked to the doctor either being in network or out of network. The former means that the care provider has a contract with certain, if not most, insurance companies. The insurance companies tell the doctor that (a) the insurance companies will bring more patients to the care provider and (b) that if the doctor does not sign an agreement, the insurance company will financially discourage patients from coming to the doctor. In return, the insurance company pays less for the service. Of course, the insurance company does *not* pass any of those savings on to the patient.

Because payment routes through an insurance company, and we've been trained for years to think more about what we pay for our insurance than we do about what medical services actually cost, your first inclination is to ask if you have met your deductible or what the co-pay is, not what the price of the service is. Alternative courses of action or providers of service, if there are any, are seldom discussed. In making healthcare decisions, not only is there an imbalance of knowledge between care provider and patient, the patient does not even know who to turn to for alternatives or even how to determine if they have other options. Again, price is never mentioned. Price is vastly different from what you pay, as we discussed in chapter 3.

This leaves the patient unable to move through the questions, answers, and analysis that would allow the patient to independently pursue a course of action other than that which has been proposed by the care provider and often through referral to an "in network" specialist, offered by the insurance company.

Okay, we have something of a problem. What happens when that problem is made worse by an economic incentive to recommend a course of action or simply take a course of action that the patient may not even know has alternatives? Marty Makary, MD, has pointed out this issue in his book *Unaccountable*. Surgeons regularly use more expensive surgical procedures that have a risk of more "complications" (which means something went wrong and will require additional medical attention and may be life-threatening) without telling the patient of the alternatives or risks because they either have an economic disincentive to learn the new technique (*e.g.,* Laparoscopy) or will be paid more for the open surgery. In fact, The Journal of The

American Medical Association published a study showing that hospitals are frequently paid more than $10,000 per complication.[2] Remember that hospital income is a function of gross billed charges.

The lack of direct payment by patient to the care provider prevents the individual patient and the collective market from learning about or exploring alternatives and challenging both price and medical opinion. Instead, we have a payment system that breeds ignorance in its participants and places the consumer's focus to what is covered rather than what is needed and at what price the service is delivered.

Median income in the United States is just over $63,000[3] and a family of four spends over $20,000 in healthcare costs *annually!*[4] Many, if not most families, do not have the cash to pay an unexpected $400 bill. (Thank goodness the car owner in the example above did not need two tires!) In fact, 70 percent of Americans have less than $1,000 saved in a savings account.[5]

Healthcare is expensive. How does the average family create savings when they are challenged with existential decisions, like get an X-ray or pay the rent; buy medicine or schoolbooks; have an operation or fix the car? If a family can't save, prosperity is elusive. If prosperity is elusive, then generational transfer of wealth is elusive. What do the children of these families learn and then model? Simply put, our overreliance on health insurance has created part of the dysfunction we experience today. So, if we need patients to pay, how do we make that possible? There are several tools designed with good intentions that are almost good . . . but not quite.

Let's take this in bites. The first bite will be a discussion of tools designed to create a pool of money that is available to that the patient to directly pay for their healthcare costs. Need an MRI? The pool of money is available. Paying cash? You pay less than the insurance company would pay. (Hint: this links to our previous discussions of pricing transparency, market forces, and patient learning.)

The second bite will be a discussion of how to fund those pools. It is neither as hard as you think, nor is the answer likely what you expect. (Flash: we call that a "teaser" to increase your interest so that you will power through the boring first bite even when it is not fun!)

The first bite goes like this. Under President George W. Bush, the federal government decided that more consumerism would be a good thing in healthcare. Now, President Bush is from Dallas, and there was a smart guy in Dallas named John Goodman who had been working in the field of healthcare policy for a long time. That's Dr. Goodman with a PhD in economics from Columbia. He agreed with the notion that more consumerism in healthcare is a good and desirable endeavor.

Here is what I like to think might have gone on. Dr. Goodman was sitting under an apple tree in Dallas . . . No, Dr. Goodman was drinking a margarita with friends in Dallas (yes, more like it) and he thought that it would be a good idea if people could save money and have the government help. The state and federal government, he figured, want folks to lead healthy lives and have access to healthcare services. Those state and federal governments have an economic interest in folks being healthy (aka "productive") and not sick (aka "not productive" and/or drawing on the state and federal government reserves known as Medicaid or Medicare or going to an already crowded "safety net" hospital paid for by county residents).

So, what if we said that anyone can take a portion of their paycheck and put it into an account dedicated to covering the costs of their healthcare, and whatever money they put into the account would not be subject to federal income tax, and in many states, it won't be subject to state income tax either. Let's also say you could earn money on whatever is in that account through interest or by investing it, and whatever you earn on investments in that account would not be not taxed either. Finally, you can spend the money in the account on healthcare goods and services without paying tax. We are going to call this "tax advantaged saving." (Hint: this is the opposite of the teaser. It is the reason we need teasers!)

That was a terrific idea! The seminal work done by Dr. John Goodman and his colleagues at the National Center for Policy Analysis and at the Goodman Institute created what we now call the Health Savings Account or HSA. Legislation creating these accounts was signed into law in December of 2003, but it still doesn't work as intended.

"Why?" you ask.

HSAs were intended to create pools of cash that could be used to pay healthcare bills. The incentive offered by government is to not tax the money you put into or take out of the accounts. The theory is that having that cash allows the patient to pay their healthcare bills directly. The money paid directly is applied to the "deductible" the patient must pay each year. That means that the insurance company does not have to pay *any* bills until the deductible has been met. In other words, the patient pays 100% of all bills until the deductible set forth in the insurance policy is met. The insurance only pays the bills after the deductible is met. If there are no bills for that year after the deductible is met the insurance company does not have to pay anything. In such case, the patient paid for all their healthcare costs directly and the insurance company has paid none of the costs, even though the insurance premium has been paid.

There is some, though not perfect, correlation between risk and the cost of the premium, meaning that if the insurance company assumes the risk of having to pay all bills greater than the deductible and less than the maximum allowed under the policy, the way to lower the cost of the premium is to increase the deductible to the greatest amount possible.

So, if you want to have the most consumerism in the marketplace and the lowest risk to the insurance company, then individuals and families should be allowed to put *as much money as possible* into their HSA and all of that HSA should be permitted to be used to pay the bills until the deductible is met. This approach allows the patient to directly pay for all expenses up to the deductible, develop a direct payment relationship with their care provider, and learn more about the care they are receiving as well as the alternatives available and the risks associated with each. Sounds good, right? So, why are only about 10 percent of Americans using HSAs?

Cynicism alert: The insurance companies are not going to let you move them out of their powerful position. You must pay insurance companies whatever premium amounts the insurance companies can convince state regulators to allow them to charge you. Even your employer has no power over the insurance companies. So, the insurance companies develop plans that do not allow you to take advantage of the HSAs in the way intended, and they lobby to diminish the HSA owner's freedom to use the money the owner has saved in the way the owner wants.

Case in point: I want to leave my HSA to my son or daughter or grandson or granddaughter when I die . . . no can do! Why not? Why would we not want to give our children or grandchildren that advantage?

Second case in point: My wife and I are allowed to contribute $7,200 ($3,600 per person) into my HSA in 2020.[6] However, under the plans offered by my insurance company, the highest available deductible is $6,600. That deductible has no correlation to the amount I am allowed to contribute to my

HSA. I cannot put the same amount of money into my HSA each year as my maximum deductible. This prevents my maximizing the tax effect of my savings and does not facilitate the maximum amount of savings. Further, when I get the HSA, I have to pay an administrative fee in addition to the amount I pay for my premium. (It is unclear if the administrative fee is deductible.) However, (Spoiler alert) the premium with the highest deductible is not materially different from the premium when my deductible was $250! The result is that I take more risk, but don't save any money.

But, let's not give up. Rather than discard the existing tools, let's review them and see if we can use them to build a better solution. Let's call it the 60% Solution!

What Is a Tax Advantage?

To be clear, I don't like talking about taxes. In fact, taxes both scare me and confuse me. I am always concerned that I will not pay the right amount, the government will audit me, and I will get chased by the IRS. To this day, I have never prepared my own tax return. I thank my CPA every year that their professional passion included tax prep!

So, with that disclosure let's work through this together. Think of it this way, you pay taxes on what is called your "modified adjusted gross income."

Start with Gross Income. Add up every single dollar and cent you make in a year as a result of working or selling something, and that is your Gross Income. This amount is not what you or the government want you to pay taxes on. Thankfully!

You "adjust" your gross income by taking permitted deductions. So, you look for opportunities to reduce the amount of tax due by taking advantage of the deductions permitted. "Permitted" is really the wrong word, because the reality is that the

US government *wants* you to take these deductions. The folks in Congress or the IRS or both have decided that it is *better* for the country and for you to take the deductions they permit than it is for you not to be able to take the deductions. In other words, the deductions are not really "permitted" but rather are "encouraged." Here is a quick example. The government wants more folks to own homes, so the interest paid on a mortgage reduces their taxable income. Here is another example: the government wants to encourage long-term investments. So, if you buy something and hold on to it for more than a year and then sell it for more than you paid for it, you pay a lower tax on the extra bit. Let's say you buy a house for $100,000, hold it for a year, and then sell it for $110,000, your tax would be less than it would be if you sold it only ten months after you purchased it.

However (and this is for the rich folks reading this), as your income increases, certain deductions are not available. When a person is deemed to have made more money than the IRS likes, the IRS changes the rules and reverses course. In other words, once you pass a certain income threshold, the IRS "disallows" some of the deductions you took to adjust your gross income downward, and thus adds back the amount you were previously able to deduct to increase your adjusted gross income. In other words, people making too much income will have a tax bill based on only adjusted gross income, which will likely be less than the tax bill based on modified adjusted gross income.

In summary, deductions are a good thing that the US government encourages you to take by creating a financial incentive for your doing so. Take the deduction and you pay less in tax. Don't take the deduction and you pay more in tax. Either way, the government has made it your call.

Clearly, if we can reduce our modified adjusted gross income, we pay less in taxes. Taking us back to healthcare expenditures, if we can save money in a way that reduces our modified adjusted gross income, that is good because we lower our tax bill. Further, if we can spend that money in a way that gives us a direct payment relationship with the care provider, that is also good, because it empowers us with knowledge and gives us bargaining power. The last two points are central to every industry in America, except, up to this point, healthcare.

The federal government has had policies in place for almost twenty years that were designed to create tax advantaged ways to save and pay for healthcare costs. There are several and each has a different set of rules. I will focus on health reimbursement accounts ("HRAs"), flexible spending accounts ("FSAs"), and health savings accounts ("HSAs"). (Don't worry, a chart is coming.)

Health Reimbursement Accounts (HRAs)

HRAs have existed in one form or another for many decades. However, rules were formalized for HRAs in 2002. Funded by the *employer,* an HRA is a tax advantaged account funded to a fixed, pre-determined amount annually at the beginning of the year that allows a company pay for certain of an employee's health expenses. Need a wheelchair? The employee can use the funds from the HRA to pay for that expense. Need dialysis? The employee can use the funds from the HRA to pay for that expense.

The important thing to note here is that the employer is funding the account, and even though the money put into the HRA benefits the employee if and to the extent used by the employee for healthcare expenses, the amount funded is not treated as taxable compensation.

Make no mistake, however, the money in the account is always the employer's money. If the employee does not use it all or if there is any portion of the HRA remaining at the end of the year, that remaining money reverts to the employer's corporate treasury. Further, the employer gets to develop the plan and determine how much to put in the HRA attributable to the employee, although the employer cannot discriminate in how much they contribute based on certain attributes of the employee. The employer, for example, cannot contribute a higher percentage to the CEO's HRA than the entry level employee's HRA.

Benefits plans are established each year and the HRA must be funded by the employer at the beginning of the year in the amount set forth in the plan for the entirety of that year. Now, depending on the company, that may be a good thing or a bad thing because for many companies there exists a seasonality to cash flows. Some companies, like retailers, have a lot of cash in the first few months of the year. Others do not. However, for those companies providing HRAs, the expense is anticipated, meaning management knows that it is going to have to fund the HRAs at a certain time of year and can plan for the expenditure. Again, funding the HRAs for the company is part of the health benefits for the company's employees.

Funds from the HRA can be used to pay an employee's health expenses, and any funds unused in one year can be rolled into the HRA for use in the following year. Now, to be clear, there is a long list of expenses that are "qualified" expenses, and you can only use money from the HRA to pay for a qualified expense. (Hint: even though the list is long and identifies many things that can be paid for by an HRA, check first in IRS Publication 502 but do not do so before driving or operating any heavy machinery.)

The good news is that qualified expenses include health insurance premiums, health insurance deductibles, coinsurance and copays, and other medical expenses, however a key determinant of expenses being "qualified" is that the expenses must be incurred within the HRA plan year. If they are not, only the HRA funding for the year in which the expense was incurred can pay for the expense.

As children have more recently lived at home longer, a question given increasing attention is whether or not benefits extend to family members up to age 26. The regulations dictate that the funds used in an HRA can be used for those family members claimed as "dependents" on your tax return.

HRAs can be offer a tax advantage certain types of companies, typically smaller companies with fewer employees. However, providing an HRA effectively limits an employee's mobility of employment. If they leave the company and don't find immediate employment elsewhere, they are again in a risky situation because the HRA funds do not follow the employee. Those funds are owned by the employer and are only available for use to pay that employer's employees. Employees who do not have a job when they leave the employer providing the HRA can apply for COBRA, but currently the HRA does not follow the employee under any circumstance, because the HRA is owned by the employer.

Flexible Spending Accounts (FSAs)

FSAs are akin to a "tweener" between the HRA and the HSA because the HRA is owned by the employer and the HSA is owned by the employee. Here's how they work. The employer establishes a benefits plan which includes FSAs. FSA funding levels are determined by the individual employee in amounts up to the limits set forth in the regulations, which are updated annually. The decision to have FSAs is that of the employer, and the decision to participate and the degree of participation in FSAs is that of the employee.

FSAs are funded through employee payroll deductions, but like HRAs, unused sums at the end of the year are returned to the employer. Recently, the regulations have changed to allow a rollover of $500, and under certain circumstances the FSA may be extended beyond the end of the year for a brief period of up to sixty days. There are other significant limitations, almost identical to those of an HRA, if the funds are not used in that particular year and if the employer leaves the company.

Under the IRS regulations, the amount an employee can contribute to an FSA is limited to $2,750 in 2020[7] and those limits are adjusted based on changes in the cost of living index. A spouse of the employee can also contribute up to $2,750. That amount is deducted pre-tax from the employee's paycheck. It is worth noting that the FSA must still reimburse any qualified medical expense even if the sum of the deductions is greater than the amount funded through payroll deductions thus far in that year.

The funds in the FSA can be used to pay deductibles and co-pays but cannot be used to pay insurance premiums. FSAs can also be used to pay for prescription and over-the-counter medicines, medical equipment, and other medical supplies. Amounts in the FSA at the end of the year are subject to one of three options selected by the employer: the FSA can either be extended by 2.5 months, $500 can be carried over to the next year, or they will be forfeited back the employer.[8] To make matters even more convenient, if you, like me, shop at places like Costco, their app will help you keep track of FSA eligible purchases.

Health Savings Accounts (HSAs)

Now, for the last of the big three—the HSA. HRAs and FSAs both provide a way to save for medical expenses and give you a tax benefit for doing so. While HRAs and FSA create a tax advantaged way for people to save for their healthcare needs, the benefit never fully transfers to the employee. If you don't use all of the HRA or FSA, the money goes back to the company. What is the incentive for the employee? One might assert that the incentives are to "use it or lose it" along with the associated tax savings at the end of the year if you are close enough to the full expenditure of funds.

By contrast, the HSA is the employee-owned pre-tax solution that is the best answer developed to date. However, as I am certain Dr. Goodman would agree, the current rules on HSAs do not go far enough in providing the needed changes to re-instill the employee with the market power and market knowledge that patients started to see go away in 1944.

What is an HSA?

Put into law under President George W. Bush, an HSA is an account into which individuals and others put money on a pre-tax basis. Note that this is the first approach we have discussed that allows for contributions to the plan by individuals other than the employee. In fact, anyone can contribute to an individual's HSA. The beneficiary of the HSA is not the only one who can contribute to the HSA, as parents, other relatives, and unrelated parties can contribute.

The money in the HSA account can be invested in virtually any form of investment vehicle: stocks, bonds, a 401(k), or any other investment vehicle. Any earnings from the invested amount that are retained in the account are not taxed, and the money spent on qualified medical expenses is not taxed. The account is owned by the employee, and all funds not used in one year can be rolled forward into the following year into perpetuity with no taxation. That is actually the point of the

HSA, to build a long-term pool of cash to be used for healthcare needs. If the employee leaves the company, the HSA goes with the employee, because the employee owns it. When the owner of the account passes away, the funds can [only] be left to his or her spouse.

There are a few limitations on the HSA, as currently structured. First, in order to qualify for an HSA, the account holder must have a high deductible health plan or HDHP. A plan is considered an HDHP if the deductible, also known as the amount that has to be paid by the employee before the insurance company pays any of the bills, is $1,350 for an individual or $2,700 for a couple. The primary rationale for the legislation enabling HSAs is that this form of tax incented savings coupled with cash payments from and controlled by the patient would introduce more consumerism into healthcare. Second, any funds that account has when the holder passes can only be left to the spouse. However, very notably, after you reach the age of sixty-five, you can withdraw funds for non-medical expenses from your HSA without penalty. In this case, while you may be taxed on the withdrawal as income and taxed at the ordinary income rate, there is no penalty.

Looking closely at the differences between the HRA, FSA, and HSA, you might quickly reach a conclusion that you might like to mix and match.

Whether your employer sets up an HRA is not your call and is likely to be a decision that is out of your control; however, you could decide to use an FSA and an HSA at the same time, as they can be used for different purposes. Generally, we might think of FSAs as a tool to pay for the costs of medical consumables, such as medicines and durable medical equipment. The FSA can be used to take care of many medical expenses from Advil to wheelchairs.[9] An FSA can also be used to pay for dental and vision costs. However, because you cannot keep the money if you don't use it, you must be cautious not to overfund the account.

What the literature will not tell you but what the more pragmatic though less scrupulous might tell you is that even though it is not allowable to combine FSAs and HAS beyond what was described above, the reality is that the government really has no way of knowing. To be clear, you should not do this, and you should not violate the law or regulations as fines and penalties will be sure to follow if you are caught. Instead, join the cause and support the effort to change the regulations.

At last, the Chart!

	Health Reimbursement Account	Flexible Spending Account	Health Savings Account
When was this put in place?	2002	1978	2003
Who funds the account?	Employer	Employee	Employee
Who owns the money in the account?	Employer	Employer	Employee
Can I transfer the money in the account?	No	No	Limited Yes
Can I use the money to pay for premiums?	Yes	No	No
Who gets any leftover money at the end of the year?	Employer	Employer	Employee
Can I use the money to pay for expenses of children?	Dependents	Dependents	No
Who determines how much can be put into the account?	Employer	Employee	Employee
Who limits how much can be put in each year?	Employer	IRS	IRS

Thus far, we have discussed the HRA, the FSA, and the HSA. We have discussed the structure and attributes of each. Now let's discuss how to fund them.

Funding the Account and Paying the Deductible

The first problem is how to handle the deductible. As mentioned, many Americans do not have the cash on hand to pay an unanticipated $400 obligation. (The statistics on this are suspicious, but—as they say in consulting—they are "directionally correct") How can they possibly handle an annual $1,350 deductible? The median income in the United States is $62,000, which means that HDHPs are out of reach for most Americans! In fact, only about 10 percent of those who have an HDHP and thus qualify for HSAs have them.

Again, anyone can put money into your HSA. That includes your employer. Rather than the employer funding an HRA, I would assert that it is better to put the same amount of money into an HSA for the employee since the company was going to incur the expense, it is a tax-deductible expense for the company, it enhances the company's goal of having productive employees, and it is not taxable to the employee. And, unlike the HRA, access to the money for qualified medical expenses now belongs to the employee, not the employer. Everyone wins in this model, though, of course, unspent funds do not return to the company.

Indexing for Success

In the current model, HSAs are only available to those who can afford to take advantage of them. It may be difficult for many to fund them to the desired goal. But wait, the state and federal governments should want the greatest funding of HSAs possible so that more consumerism is injected into the healthcare industry. President Bush established that consumerism in healthcare is a good thing. Dr. John Goodman showed us why consumerism in healthcare is a good thing. Dr. Jeremy Lin, author of *Myth or Magic—The Singapore Health System* said consumerism in healthcare is a good thing. Sean Flynn, professor at Scripps College and author of the book *The Cure That Works: How to Have the World's Best Health Care—at a Quarter of the Price* agrees that consumerism in healthcare is a good thing. So, let's make it a goal to fully fund HSAs for as many Americans as possible.

But there is a problem here that many do not want to discuss. The problem has implications that affect everything from mobility between the classes, a goal of the United States since inception, to democracy itself. What does a person who is the household and income producer for a family of four do when presented with a promotion or a raise that, if taken, causes the family to no longer qualify for Medicaid? Should that person lose their Medicaid coverage, bad things happen, bad for the individual, bad for the family, bad for the company, and bad for the country. Contrary to the common good, this earner is financially discouraged from taking the raise or promotion because that would mean that the earner and his or her family now must pay for their healthcare themselves. But with what money? Let's remember, the cost of healthcare insurance for a family of four averages between $20,000 and $25,000 per year.[10] The problem is that the attention to the cost of the premium is a misleadingly poor proxy for the cost of healthcare, because it does not include the deductible that must be paid by the family, nor does it include the cost of medical consumables: medicines and durable medical equipment.

The biggest swath of the American population precluded from taking advantage of HSAs are those who don't qualify for Medicaid because they make too much money to qualify for Medicaid but make less money than that required to recover the purchasing power they had when they did qualify for Medicaid. Put differently, households in Texas with an income of more than $50,980 and less than approximately $75,000, are trapped in a financial chasm. They make more than the maximum amount to qualify for Medicaid and yet do not have the purchasing power they had when they were on Medicaid. This chasm between their purchasing power while on Medicaid and what they lose at income levels just above eligibility is between 200% and 300% of the federally defined poverty level, the FPL.

Most of us don't start our careers making a large amount of money. Our first jobs may be in food services, retail, manual labor (I mowed lawns), or in some other minimum or low wage job. As we get older and move out of our family's home, we get roommates or, increasingly, we return to home to live with our parents until an age far older than the age our parents might have lived their parents' homes. While we may or may not be on Medicaid, even if we qualify, many of us live from paycheck to paycheck as *Forbes* says 78 percent of Americans do.[11]

Further, income growth does not happen in a standard or predictable fashion. Everyone does not grow, evolve, or promote out of this economic circumstance. Some employees will stay in their current position with modest annual increases for many years. Some will quit their jobs or be terminated from their jobs. Others will get promoted and stay in the promoted position with modest increases for years. A subset of those promoted will go on to further professional and income growth over time. Others will change jobs, professions, and industries. Studies now show that the average person changes careers six times in their life!

We don't all have equal access to all opportunities and, to paraphrase Ken Wilber from *Integral Psychology*, we are all born with the sum of all attributes of all humans, but we develop them at different rates of speed and in different volumes. That is what makes us different people. This is true not only of our psychological composition but also our professional competencies.

Some have the aptitude or fundamental capability to be an employee but not a supervisor, or to be a supervisor but not a manager, or to be a manager but not a CEO.

Noting that there exists movement, up and down, in income is important. We start our earning in one place and then change jobs, add more education or training, get a raise, get promoted, change careers, or lose our job. Looking at the household with income that is the maximum allowed to get Medicaid is to be faced with a grave reality. What does that person do when a positive economic event, getting a raise or promotion, causes that household to no longer qualify for Medicaid? The average four-person household spends approximately $20,000 to $25,000 per year on healthcare, including insurance, deductibles, co-pays, medicines, medical supplies, and medical equipment. We need a bridge to encourage, assist, and incent household earners to help them through the financial chasm that is 200% to 300% of the federal poverty level.

The 60% Solution calls for what I am calling indexing of benefits. Let's break this down into two parts. A family of four will get a benefit, let's call it the Health Incentive Benefit. To get the benefit, the family will have to contribute to an HSA. The amount they contribute, or the Family Contribution, each year is to be matched by the government. The amount of the match would be determined by a multiplier that changes based on the household income of that family. Let's call the multiplier the Solution Index. Mathematically,

Health Incentive Benefit = Family Contribution multiplied by the Solution Index.

Without getting to the specifics, imagine a family contributed $25 each month and the Solution Index was 6, then for every month the family contributes $25, the government puts $150 into the HSA: $25 + $150 = $175. If this is done for a full year, the total is 12 X $175 or $2,100 which is more than enough to qualify for a HDHP. This gives purchasing power back to the individual and should lower the cost of the insurance premium because the higher deductible has the effect of reducing risk for the insurance carrier, all good things.

The Solution Index will change depending on the household income between 200% of FPL, above which the family no longer qualifies for Medicaid, and 300% of FPL, the amount at which the loss of purchasing power associated with ineligibility for Medicaid is overcome.

This approach creates more consumers exerting considerably more market power on the industry and will allow those in this stratum of the US population to benefit in many important ways, which will have a domino effect for every other partic-ipant in the industry. As patients have money to directly pay their care providers, patients will learn more about their health needs, alternative solutions, and make risk-adjusted decisions.

This approach encourages people to leave Medicaid, which is good for the healthcare industry, as doctors typically lose money at the Medicaid reimbursement rates. It also will save governments a great deal of money or and allow them to reallocate those resources to satisfy the same needs better or satisfy other needs not addressed.

Consumerism in healthcare is a good thing. Creating more consumers with cash to pay for goods and services does not mean that they will pay more for each product or service, but it does mean that they will understand what things cost and potentially can negotiate prices directly just as Medicaid does. Yes, this can happen.

Let me get it out there first, I have heard very, very high-ranking executives say very dismissive things about Amer-icans as consumers in healthcare. The comment I have heard that offends me most is that Americans are either not smart enough or not well informed enough to be consumers of health-care. *Nothing could be further from the truth!* This has proven not to be the case in any industry. Do I know what the chemical composition of automobile tires is? No. Did I buy some last week after carefully comparison shopping online? Yes!

Critics who find the "consumer is too ignorant" argument fails will often quickly pivot to "who is going to pay for this Indexing thing?" Certainty of payment mentioned earlier in this text comes from the change in taxation of benefits which costs the US treasury over $400 billion per year. Industry costs will be significantly reduced through the effects of consumerism, direct payment and elimination of administrative costs, which in turn effect projections from the CBO on future healthcare costs currently in the Medicaid and Medicare budget forecasts and reduce our real federal deficit.

Finally, how do we provide a way for people on Medicaid to avoid the characterization or reality of being a member of the "working poor"? We are not supposed to be economically or financially trapped by the market or by regulation or by other forms of oppression, much less trapped by growing success. Our democracy and our economic system are premised on the notion that there is no limitation to what one can do with their hard work and talents, and it is logical that most of us reach higher levels of income incrementally. There is or should be no entrenchment in any socio-economic class. In fact, in our society we abhor the notion of a class system altogether. Instead, we want people to improve their lives. We want people to grow their income. We want people to increase their wealth. We want people to decrease their risk. We want individual responsibility, and we want our children to do better than we've done. That requires good health, physically and financially. It also requires less worry about financial ruin because we don't have enough of the current brand of health insurance. While it is difficult to determine how many individuals and families are forced into bankruptcy due to the healthcare costs of a major medical problem, it has been suggested that a substantial percentage of bankruptcies are healthcare related. The reality is that healthcare problems may lead to an inability to work, which leads to an inability to pay bills while still incurring normal living expenses plus the costs of addressing the illness or medical issue itself.

Let's consider the family of Pat and Lynne. If we could encourage those earners to save $25 a month into an HSA and match that with funds from state and federal government coffers also placed into that HSA so that the funds in the HSA in the first year in which they get the full index is sufficient to pay the deductible for their HDHP for that year, they could move into the commercial insurance market, have good coverage, and begin exerting market force on the industry.

We can go further though. I suggest that the index should start at 150%, though not be accessible with a match of 4:1 meaning that every $1 contributed by the individual is matched by $4 in state and federal funds. If an earner can save $25 per month for a year, they would contribute $300 for the year. Matching their contribution with the government contribution at a rate of 4:1 would mean that the HSA would have an additional $1,200 for a total in the HSA of $1,500. The 60% Solution provides that for every year the individual contributes, the individual gets the match. Again, these funds can only be accessed when they have an HDHP and can only be used for qualified medical expenses. The matching amount would be reduced based on the household's relation to the FPL. Household income of 200% of FPL would get the same 4:1 match, but the match would move to 3:1 at 250% of FPL, and there would be no match from for earners making more than 300% of FPL.

Remember, while there is a cap on how much one can put into the HSA and get the tax advantages on the contributed amount, there is no cap on the amount of money that can accrue and stay in the HSA, and the HSA can roll all unused funds forward and invest them as the owner chooses. This feature encourages people to be thoughtful about using the funds in the HSA while at the same time having the absence of stress that comes from knowing they can pay their healthcare bills. Of course, that those funds can be used on children of HSA owners, can be left to the HSA of the spouse and, expanding on the current rules, be left to the children of the HSA owner. This allows for faster progress for younger Americans to get to financial and economic health. In other words, the domino effect of The 60% Solution is or could be a wealth transfer opportunity for members of those newly able to take advantage of an HSA.

To sum, there are several important recommendations here. First, allow the combining of FSAs and HSAs to allow the existing tax advantaged incentives of these plans to be fully realized by more people. This creates more consumerism, which is a good thing. Second, create incentives to encourage more of our population to use fully funded HSAs. Third, create an "indexed" matching program that builds an offramp for those currently on Medicaid and allows people to avoid financially suffering when they no longer qualify for Medicaid.

Let us now return from our dream and imagine waking up in a new world. In this world, a greater percentage of Americans have more control over their bodies and their health. In this world, a greater percentage of Americans have more control over their money and what they spend it on. In this world, a greater percentage of Americans have more ability to move from poor to working class and leap over the moniker of "working poor." In this world, a greater percentage of Americans have greater understanding about their health.

Chapter Six
CHANGE GOVERNANCE

Access to the medical profession is so heavily regulated that the games played to get into medical school begin long before a college transcript is sent, the MCAT is taken, or an eligible student begins the laborious interview process. In fact, often it isn't even good enough to get into just any medical school, which is an amazing accomplishment, but instead, one must get into the "right" medical school, as this will directly influence what residencies and internships the student might secure after graduating from medical school. Just like any other profession, biases proliferate.

A skeptic might conclude that the medical schools themselves are designed far more for the economic benefit of the institution and the profession it serves than the education of the student. A recent conversation with a current medical school student aspiring to be an orthopedic surgeon confirmed my observations over the years, as he said that he could easily finish his remaining classes in 2 months but would have to spend 14 more months in school. Most professional schools pack 1–2 years of education into 3–4 years of school, which reflects the reality that most students in professional schools are incredibly bright and accomplished. Few of them are there to enjoy beer pong and frat parties. Unless, of course, they are trying to stretch 1–2 years of school into 3–4 years.

We have long since accepted the academic and clinical sequence of medical education and the effort required to complete it as just the way it is for men and women who desire to become doctors. As we've seen though, it has not always been this way. Prior to the early 1900s, there were a variety of ways to become a doctor in a variety of fields all calling themselves medicine. States did not really regulate the educational requirements for becoming a doctor, the licensing of physicians, the practice of medicine, or the broader healthcare industry. Further, none of them consistently required any semblance of the empirical method in teaching science and all of them included some form of "academic" or other training of some sort, though not necessarily or consistently any licensing.

It would be convenient to dismiss the model of the early 1900s or any other model as all good or all bad. Instead, examination of the model yields insights into both. It is almost always useful to ask, "how did we get here?" So, let's take it all the way back to the aforementioned Abraham Flexner.

The Impact of Abraham Flexner

Like many children of first-generation immigrants coming to the United States in the late nineteenth century, Abraham Flexner was born into a large family full of hope and the American dream. He was the first in his family to complete high school and go on to college.[1] In 1886, at age nineteen and only two years after he began his studies, Flexner completed a Bachelor of Arts at Johns Hopkins University. His rapid achievement of his degree was clearly a sign of notable things to come. He later pursued degrees in psychology both at Harvard and the University of Berlin but never completed those degrees.[2]

Flexner returned to Louisville to teach at a private school. Given that Flexner had completed his undergraduate degree in only two years, it is perhaps not surprising that he regarded the academic system as broken. Four years after returning to Louisville, he started his own school to fulfill his vision of focusing on the individual student and employing unique methods of teaching that included no standard curriculum, small learning groups, no exams, no academic records, and considerable project work. His model gave his students recognition and acceptance at well-regarded colleges and universities.[3]

One might call Mr. Flexner an activist educator. Flexner published his first book, *The American College,* in 1908. His dedication to the concept of an education centered on the needs and aptitudes of the individual was in stark contrast, he found, to American colleges and universities at the time, more interested in promoting a rigid curriculum delivered to large classes through lecture. His book argued that higher education was unduly concerned with research and profitability to the detriment of its educational mission.[4]

The American College was well received, importantly by Henry Pritchett. Mr. Pritchett was president of the vaunted Carnegie Foundation. Soon, the two met and Mr. Pritchett commissioned Mr. Flexner to lead a study of 155 American and Canadian medical schools. Mind you, Mr. Flexner had never attended a single day of medical school, so his observations were, shall we say, *de novo.* His findings were published in 1910 under the eponymous title, "The Flexner Report."

As with our reading any other report from long ago, we find things important, less important, and horrifying when we view Flexner's comments through a contemporary lens. We cannot ignore the character of the times in which he wrote, but we also cannot ignore the enduring application of some of Flexner's findings and the long reach of some of his recommendations.

Mr. Flexner and his team concluded that there were no effective medical licensing laws either at the state or federal level. This implied that unqualified or underqualified "entrepreneurs" were practicing medicine. Keep in mind, the research for and publication of the Flexner report was done following the culmination of the great industrial revolution. Science, math, engineering, physics, and other disciplines were flourishing. The electric light had led to advances with the microscope. Photography was being used in fields ranging from psychology to surgery. Refrigeration led to treatments of yellow fever. The tabulating machine introduced what we now call data processing. The hearing aid was invented in 1902.

All of this innovation was possible because of experimentation, trial and error and, more importantly, the empirical method. The empirical method dictated that math and science be used to create consistent, measurable experiments. If the outcomes of consistent tests were the same, then one could derive conclusions about that which was observed. More importantly, professionals with similar training seeing that the same data producing the same outcome would reach the same conclusions.

The empirical method was the opening Flexner needed to fundamentally transform and shape healthcare for the next century and beyond. In fact, his report continues to influence every aspect of healthcare, starting with education. He was the first to assert that doctors should not only have to go to medical school but those seeking admission to medical schools should get a degree from an undergraduate school before going to a four-year medical school. Borrowing from his success with the Flexner School, he asserted that the medical school curriculum should include physical experiences, like dissections, and be a part of a larger research university. Further, he advocated for standardization of medical school curricula and greater use of the scientific method and reasoning, and he placed greater emphasis on laboratory sciences.

While Flexner's report was making great impact across the nation in the field of medical education, Sir William Osler was also contributing to the need for additional training for physicians. A giant in the field of medicine, Osler wrote many books, taught at a number of universities, and had diseases, treatments, and buildings named after him. Most notably, he developed the first scientific textbook for medicine and the first residency program for medical students. This was the first time that students would see patients under the supervision of a licensed physician at the patient's bedside. This was a perfect complement to Flexner's recommendation for lab work.[5] The lab work was project oriented research while the bedside visits were practical, patient-centered research.

Osler was a founder of John Hopkins Hospital and later taught at Oxford, leading to his being knighted. His focus was patient-centric care and he was famously quoted as saying "The good physician treats the disease; the great physician treats the patient who has the disease."[6]

He also advocated for the "ethical physician."[7]

Over the next two decades, change in medical education happened quickly. Medical schools were streamlined and homogenized or closed altogether. Most American institutions granting MD or DO degrees were closed within the first two decades following Flexner's report. For those that advanced, new curricula were added, new facilities were created, and substantial qualitative gains were made across healthcare. The quality of physicians was, generally, greatly improved. Penicillin was developed. New treatments emerged. It's important to recall that this was happening at a time when fewer than 10% of patients had health insurance and most patients paid their caregivers directly.

As with any broad-based advancement, all outcomes of Flexner's critique were not equally good. In fact, some very negative outcomes manifested. Flexner vilified any approach to medicine that did not advocate the use of treatments such as vaccines to prevent and cure illness as tantamount to quackery and charlatanism. This stigmatized osteopathic medicine, chiropractic medicine, electrotherapy, eclectic medicine, naturopathy, and homeopathy among others. Flexner advocated for the closing of all but two historically black medical schools and his success in that effort led to a vast undersupply of physicians of color, particularly in demographically determined areas. The devastating effect of this has spread across decades of care. As we've seen, to this day, despite the fact that African Americans comprise approximately 13 percent of the population, only 4 percent of active physicians are black, and Flexner's influence in this situation is undeniable when we note that nearly 80 percent of those physicians were educated at one of the two schools that survived Flexner's analysis.[8] This has led to ongoing "medical deserts" popping up where physicians of color have retired and their clinics closed when there were no doctors of color available to replace them. Medical education became more expensive and more exclusive as a result. The geographic distribution of doctors around the country became concentrated as the number of doctors interested in working in rural areas declined. Family medicine practices were harmed.

At the same time, governmental regulation was dramatically stepped up. Flexner advocated that state grant permission for the creation and establishment of the size of medical schools. While he advocated that each state branch of the American Medical Association have oversight over the conventional medical schools within their state, in the interest of homogeneity, he advocated that medical schools adhere to the rules of the American Association of Medical Colleges.

The influence of Flexner's commentaries does not stop there. Once a student graduates from medical school, the student pursues licensing. Licensure is a process that takes place at the state level in accordance with each state's laws. All states require that applicants for MD licensure be graduates of an approved medical school and complete the United States Medical Licensing Exam ("USMLE"). This standard remains today. One might ask why you must attend an accredited school if you still need to take the exam. Once again, we must ask: what is the purpose of accreditation?

People who earned their medical degrees in other countries must satisfy these requirements before practicing medicine in the United States. However, the issue of where a physician graduated from medical school influences those states in which the physician can get licensed. This raises interesting questions on matters of the use of technology to do all manner of things: read lab test results, offer diagnoses, and "see" patients or use telemedicine. Telemedicine has been heralded as a solution to the rising cost of healthcare, the argument being that we can use telemedicine to reach underutilized or lower cost providers in other states or countries to deliver the same or better service at a lower price.

"The Trained Nurse is One of the Blessings of Humanity"[9]

Flexner's report also held great influences over the career of nursing. Flexner defined a "profession" as one that had the following characteristics:

1. Professions involve essentially intellectual operations with large individual responsibility.

2. They derive their raw material from science and learning.

3. This material they work up to a practical and definite end.

4. They possess an educationally communicable technique (their own language).

5. They tend to self-organization.

6. They are becoming increasingly altruistic in motivation.[10]

While nurses concluded they met these qualifications, the practice of nursing had been characterized into a variety of licenses:

- Licensed Vocational Nurse where the requirement is a one-year diploma or certificate program from an accredited school and passing the National Council Licensure Examination for Practical Nursing ("NCLEX-PN"). Licensure allows the recipient to change dressings and handle other wound care functions, check vitals, administer medications, bathe patients and help with other activities of daily living, work in nursing care facilities, and work under the supervision of physicians and registered nurses.

- Registered Nurse where the requirement is a two-year or a four-year degree from an accredited school and passing the National Council Licensure Examination for Registered Nurses ("NCLEX-RN"). Licensure allows the recipient to administer medications, perform life support functions, admit and discharge patients, perform wound care, develop care plans, and perform other functions under the supervision of a physician.

A Century after Flexner and Osler

There are also specialties for nurses, including, being a certified nurse anesthetist, a certified nurse practitioner, a certified nurse midwife, a clinical nurse specialist, and others. Each has its own additional educational and licensing requirements.

The advent of telemedicine presents a concern as to how to handle state licensure issues when medical care is being shared between states through telecommunications. In fact, by current laws, reimbursement requirements and allowances for telemedicine continue as a state-by-state mystery to be solved. The states always require that the provider be licensed in the state where the person lives. If the patient lives in California, the provider must be acting under the direction of a physician licensed by the state of California, but the laws require far more granularity to determine if requirements are met. Will the service be delivered in a synchronous manner (live telephone call, video call, or other real-time two-way communication technology) or in and asynchronous context (email, fax, voicemail, or some other communication technology)? Has consent been properly obtained for information to be shared and is there full disclosure that the remote caregiver is in another state? The laws may require posting specific disclosures on websites, or notices at the desk in the office or some other form of conspicuous notice.[11] Though he never imagined telemedicine, the remaining legacy of Flexner is the long-standing state licensing requirement.

States continue to grapple with the issue of cross-border service provision. If the patient lives in Virginia and the doctor lives in North Carolina, in which state must the physician be licensed? This question, another legacy of Flexner, is relevant whether or not telemedicine is involved and affects not only the legal provision of services, but also informs many payment issues. Medicaid and Medicare rules may differ from rules relating to private insurance, and, again, this is a state-by-state issue. California law, for example, states that an insurance company cannot compel a face-to-face visit if a telemedicine visit will deliver the service; however, the patient must be in the state and the physician must be licensed by the state. Some states have recently established procedures for recognizing the licenses of physicians practicing in other states in times of emergency, such as after hurricanes or earthquakes.

Thus, licensing remains critical to delivering healthcare service in any jurisdiction and to getting paid for delivering that service. These are two different things. Just because you are licensed does not mean you are going to be paid. There are myriad other matters to deal with regarding payment, and some of them have been expanded upon in chapter 3, but let's stick with licensing for the purposes of this discussion.

"Examinations Hinder Rather than Foster Learning"[12]

To be clear, getting licensed is far more arduous than applying for medical school. Applying to medical school is the culmination of undergraduate work, taking the MCAT, filing out and submitting applications, paying the fees, and visiting schools. Expensive? Yes, but compared to the effort of licensing, a walk in the park.

If our goal is to increase the supply and diversity of doctors throughout the country, the first step is to streamline the education process. It should not take so many years of education to become a doctor. Does the AMA really want to tell me that taking undergraduate electives is critical to getting a license to practice medicine? Further, does one really need to attend an accredited school *and* take the state exam to be licensed? One of those two has to go.

It is not just that more doctors are needed, it is that far more are needed. And, whatever is needed is different on a state-by-state basis. In Texas, for example, a person seeking to become a doctor must first have an undergraduate degree to be admitted to medical school, graduate from an accredited medical school, apply for, obtain, and complete a residency, apply for, obtain, and complete an internship, and this is all before they can apply to sit for the state licensing exam that they must pass. The applicant must also have a Board certification. In addition to the state exam, there are additional federal requirements that the states have adopted or that federal laws have mandated. Applicants must pass the United States Medical Licensing Exam ("USMLE") Steps 1 to 3, and, as a requirement of HIPAA, obtain a National Provider Identifier (Type 1) issued by the Centers for Medicaid and Medicare Services.[13] Then, the graduate may apply.

Well, almost . . . the applicant must apply for, take, and pass the jurisprudence exam which makes certain the applicant is sufficiently aware of applicable laws related to the practice of healthcare. They must also apply for and get an account with the Licensure Inquiry System of Texas, provide fingerprints, and provide a criminal history report.[14] Perhaps my favorite line in all the research performed for this book is this seemingly innocent question, "Why? The NPI is an Administrative Simplification mandate of HIPAA."[15]

Of course, don't forget your liability insurance.

It makes perfect sense that this educational, licensing, and regulatory gauntlet would understandably give rise to a sense of superiority and elitism among those who persevere through the maze of requirements. Sir William Osler anticipated this and was quoted as saying:

Physicians should be wary of professional arrogance. Perhaps no sin so easily besets us as a sense of self-satisfied superiority to others. It cannot always be called pride, that master sin, but more often is an attitude of mind which either leads to bigotry and prejudice or to such a vaunting conceit in the truth of one's own beliefs and positions, that there is no room for tolerance of ways and thoughts which are not as ours are.[16]

The sad fact is that all these rules, requirements, and regulations do not guarantee good doctors. It may, in fact, create bad doctors. In 1996 HIPAA included a feature that

> created the Health Care Fraud and Abuse Control Program, a far-reaching program to combat fraud and abuse in healthcare, including both public and private health plans. As was the case before HIPAA, amounts paid to Medicare in restitution or for compensatory damages must be deposited in the Medicare Trust Funds. The Act requires that an amount equaling recoveries from healthcare investigations—including criminal fines, forfeitures, civil settlements and judgments, and administrative penalties—also be deposited in the Trust Funds.[17]

The reports Office of the Inspector General also point out that the return on investment for combatting fraud and abuse is quite good. For every $1.00 the US government spends on this effort, the Department of Justice collects, not wins or is awarded but collects, $4.00.[18] Any investor would be happy with that, and the numbers are staggering. If you add the numbers in the annual reports since inception, and read the reports themselves, you would quickly learn that the Department of Justice has won approximately $30 billion in awards![19]

There has been no safe quarter in the effort to combat fraud and abuse. In fact, county hospitals, large hospital systems, independent hospitals, for-profit hospitals, not-for-profit hospitals, pharmaceutical firms, durable medical equipment providers, pharmacies, dentists, insurance companies, physicians, physician practices, anesthetists, nurses, home healthcare providers, hospice providers, and other have all paid fines, penalties, civil settlements, or gone to prison. Step back for a moment and let that sink in. Virtually every type of provider, for-profit, not-for-profit, publicly traded, private, or otherwise, has been prosecuted and has had to pay penalties of one kind or another the federal or state government as a result of that prosecution. For example, the large safety-net county hospital called "Parkland," which was long ago made famous as being the place where President Kennedy was taken after he was shot in Dallas, had to pay a civil settlement of approximately $1.4 million.[20] That is right. A county hospital, known as one of the best hospitals in the country, was prosecuted by the federal government for fraud. Not the physicians who practiced there, but the hospital itself.

Possibly contributing to this abuse is the complexity of the claims themselves which, in addition to diagnosis codes, also include a Current Procedure Terminology ("CPT") code, that is published and updated annually by the American Medical Association. They are used to document the procedures performed by the doctor's office in response to the diagnosis and condition of the patient as described in the ICD codes discussed above. Finally, there is a last set of codes known as HCPCS or healthcare common procedure coding system, which augment the CPT codes by addressing the payment obligations related to additional services, durable medical equipment, and other goods and services that may not be included in the CPT.[21]

It is easy to now see why so many get in so much trouble with civil and criminal liability. The number of codes, the interoperability of the codes, and the ease with which one can intentionally or unintentionally get it wrong is statistically incalculable. In addition to the approximately $30 billion awarded, there are countless other investigations, lawsuits, disputed claims, delayed payments, and related administrative tasks that we, the American public, are paying for through inflated healthcare prices and correspondingly inflated insurance premiums.

I don't mind or care if the insurance companies and every other player in the healthcare industry makes a fair profit and pays their people market rates. In fact, they should. What I take objection to is the needless waste emanating like a stench out of the compost pile called our healthcare system. The price we individually and collectively pay is a lack of conformity, a lack of supply, a great number of lawsuits, increased patient dissatisfaction, and reduced capital that could be deployed towards greater or more rapid advances in the health and quality of life for every person in our nation.

The focus of this chapter has been to show how regulations and licensing create limitations in the delivery system of healthcare that drive up costs. Additionally, they serve as a barrier to creating a greater supply of doctors. Unsurprisingly, while the quality of our caregivers is terrific, we do not score well in any of the following categories ranking the supply of various caregivers:

- Doctors per 1,000—around 40th in the world;[22]

- Hospital beds per 1,000—around 80th in the world;[23]

- Nurses per 1,000—about 16th in the world.[24]

Of greatest concern is this statistic: The United States has the highest maternal death rate in the developed world according to a study by *USA Today*.[25]

"Medicine is a science of uncertainty and an art of probability."[26]

Pharmacy Is the Art of Profit

Let's not ignore the problem with pharmaceutical companies and the out-of-control world of prescription drug pricing. Yes, they do have to do a lot of research and they do have to run through the very expensive and very time-consuming gauntlet of Federal Drug Administration approval. Yes, they need to recover their investment to develop drugs and deserve to earn a fair return given their risk. However, much of this is wildly misleading. Many drugs remain under patent protection for years through minor chemical modifications that do not provide meaningful improvement in treating the illnesses they are allegedly trying to address.

The mission statement of the FDA is "The Food and Drug Administration (FDA) is responsible for protecting the public health by assuring the safety, efficacy, and security of human and veterinary drugs, biological products, medical devices, our nation's food supply, cosmetics, and products that emit radiation. The FDA also provides accurate, science-based health information to the public."[27] More specifically related to drugs, the FDA's Center for Drug Evaluation and Research "ensures that safe and effective drugs are available to improve the health of the people in the United States." However, we learn daily of medicines that cause more problems than they cure, are available but not prescribed as generics, or that are available outside of the United States at a fraction of the cost in the United States. The FDA should allow physicians greater autonomy in their prescriptions, which would solve many of these problems. Further, the United States should have a "most favored nations" clause or regulation for government program purchases to allow prescription drugs to be purchased in the United States for the lowest price offered.

Accountability for Care

Another persistent healthcare problem is that there is no real accountability for physicians. A modest amount of financial pain is imposed on the physician if complications arise out of surgeries, for example. This comes in the form of declined physician charges for follow-up visits or subsequent related surgical procedures. Fewer problems occur where we have patients whose problem has not been resolved on the initial visit. Peer reviews are largely ineffective, as there exists a staggering degree of professional courtesy granted in these reviews. Still, in the surgical example, peer reviews seldom lead to loss of privileges at a hospital, and even if loss of privileges were an effective sanction, many, if not most, surgeons have privileges at more than one hospital, further minimizing any negative impact the loss of privileges at one hospital might have had on the incompetent or negligent surgeon.

In his book *Unaccountable,* Marty Makary refers to a representational "Dr. Hodad" and points out a few things that are surprisingly terrifying. First, the name "Hodad" is an acronym that refers to "Hands Of Death And Destruction" and refers to a fictional doctor who represents the worst of medicine, and who sadly has clones in many if not all healthcare systems in the United States (and maybe the world). He is known by the moniker because of his terrible track record of surgeries botched over and over. Even more troubling is the lack of oversight Dr. Hodad, and most other surgeons and virtually all other doctors, actually receive. Still worse yet, is the asymmetry of knowledge between the patient and Dr. Hodad. No one tells the patient of this doctor's history or track record. As a result, shockingly, despite terrible surgical skills, despite devastating outcomes, and despite numerous surgical complications, the patient may believe he or she is lucky to have had the outcome produced. "Thank you for amputating my leg during my gall bladder surgery, Dr. Hodad. You saved my life!" No, Dear Patient, Dr. Hodad actually erred so badly during the procedure that the leg had to be removed because of the poor practices and terrible quality of healthcare rendered. The tone of these words fails to communicate the very outrage that I feel or the reader should share!

Two broad issues come to mind. First, most things done in a clinical setting are *not* based on science, but rather they are based on statistical probability or, alternatively, on "gut feel." A study done by Mark H. Ebell, Randi Sokol, Aaron Lee, Christopher Simons, and Jessica Early published by the National Library of Medicine[28] concluded that only 18% of a physician's recommended course of action is based on patient-oriented evidence.[29] Despite the industry's ambition to standardize everything, this is not happening. One cannot tell future doctors they are invincible deities in medical school and then expect them to subordinate their diagnosis and care plan to that of someone they have never met or seen. In fact, a recent study concluded "that patients received 54.9% of recommended care, that the proportion of recommended care slightly differed for preventive, acute, and chronic care, and that differences were even larger for different medical functions (screening, diagnosis, treatment and follow-up)."[30]

In a paper entitled "Compromised Compliance with Evidence-Based Guidelines" researchers found that ob-gyn, cardiology, general practice, emergency medicine, trauma, intensive care, oncology, and other practice areas all consistently failed to comply with guidelines more than half the time.[31] The problem is not just failure to comply with guidelines but the guidelines themselves. While I am unyielding in my belief that the United States has the best healthcare practitioners in the world, we can get better. Evidence-based medicine is the logical corollary to Flexner's report with Osler's contributions. Flexner asserted in 1910 that few medical schools taught science-based medicine and further advocated the rigorous implementation of the empirical method. Evidence-based medicine is the progeny of the integration of the empirical method in healthcare.

These and over a hundred other studies I reviewed across the spectrum of medical specialties collectively and strongly suggest that large proportions of medical clinical practice demonstrate low to at most modest compliance with evidence-based recommendations and practice guidelines. Aggravating this problem is the related—and underlying—problem, of clinical practice being informed by putative evidence-based clinical practice guidelines that themselves are of significantly compromised methodological quality.[32]

Billing claims also include a CPT code, or Current Procedure Terminology code, that is published and updated annually by the American Medical Association. They are used to document the procedures performed by the doctor's office in response to the diagnosis and condition of the patient as described in the ICD discussed codes above. The last set of codes are those known as the Health Care Common Procedure Coding System ("HCPCS"), which augment the CPT codes by addressing the payment obligations related to additional services, durable medical equipment, and other goods and services not included in the CPT.[30]

What Will Work?

As I suggested earlier the first step toward improving the supply and quality of doctors must be a change in the educational requirements of doctors. The curriculum needs to be streamlined and the examinations need only to be taken by those *not* attending an accredited medical school.

A second element of the Solution is the elimination of state licenses. This will be controversial, but the accreditation function is already being performed by a national body with national standards. Human beings do not vary in structure or composition from one state to another, so there is no reason for the additional requirement of state-by-state licensure. The elimination of state licenses leads then to the elimination of restrictions emanating from one state that prevent a physician or other healthcare provider from practicing in another state. This will increase the quality of care and increase competition among providers by allowing the markets to function more freely.

The heavily regulated healthcare industry by itself is problematic in creating administrative complexity and cost, limiting the supply of caregivers, and creating very perverse economic incentives for all in the industry. However, our system is worse than that. We have state regulation, federal regulation and, in some instances, additional regulation at the city and county levels. Still further, we have additional forms of regulation when hospitals are housed in municipal or hospital districts. That needlessly complex structure has a negatively synergistic effect because, unsurprisingly, the regulations do not always work in concert or may outrightly conflict with each other. As a nation, we should recognize that we have evolved beyond the largely agrarian models that mandated licenses be correlated to state boundaries.

There exist countless research reports, indices, and other expert findings that unequivocally conclude that the more regulation that exists in a market or industry, the less efficient that market or industry becomes. Even quick reading of reports coming from The Mercatus Center, The Fraser Institute, The Heritage Foundation, The Cato Institute, The Mises Institute, The Niskanen Center, The Adam Smith Institute, The American Enterprise Institute, The Hoover Institution, and many others outside of the United States quickly prove this point. This is not to say that no regulation is the desired end state, but rather that excessive or bad regulation is counterproductive.

Worse yet, this combination of commercial and governmental regulation has artificially created a greater distance between the patient and the caregiver. Private entities like the American Medical Association and its affiliates control the education and licensing of caregivers. Our move towards globalism has allowed the intrusion into the US healthcare system of non-US regulatory bodies like the World Health Organization who influence everything from data collection to coding for billing purposes. We have also not only allowed, but compelled, hospital systems through protocols and insurance companies through coding and policies to become *de facto* regulators in determining what healthcare is, how much healthcare will be paid for, and what types of healthcare is paid for. Consider further that the cost of healthcare premiums is so great that even if a patient wanted to purchase services not covered by their plan, they would not be likely to have the funds to do so. This matter is particularly acute for those financially just outside of Medicaid coverage.

The 60% Solution moves back to market freedom, promotes better exchange of information, allows more freedom for the individual to make decisions, and will necessarily drive down the cost of healthcare for the entire industry, benefitting not only those with insurance but also benefitting those with Medicare and Medicaid. Injecting more consumerism into the payment process is good on all accounts and really hurts no one in the process. The 60% Solution encourages caregivers to operate more efficiently, adopt technology, use the adopted technology, improve business processes, and follow other good business practices. In return, healthcare providers are rewarded with dramatically improved cash flow and improved margins. Our current form of governance is uniformly bad, producing a managerial drag across the industry that limits access, ensures sub-optimal outcomes, and creates a drag on profit.

Chapter Seven
THE VERY NEAR FUTURE OF HEALTHCARE

Perhaps the most narcissistic of exercises, aside from the belief that anyone actually wants to read it, is to assert that they, too, might complete, in whole or in part, the great start to Martin Luther King's most well-known speech of all time: "I have a dream . . ." For me to assume that my thoughts can contribute to that brilliant prose is both folly and bravado. Rather than attempt to do so, I would hope that my efforts may inspire others to not only share my view, but catalyze those in positions of consequence in policy or commerce to take up the discussion of the all-important topic of healthcare in our country, to implore with urgency that the 60% Solution is worthy of serious consideration and possibly adoption.

The current healthcare system is far too expensive, ineffective, and unresponsive to our nation's current needs; it violates the moral and ideological tenets we hold dear as a nation; and it is incapable of timely response to epidemic or pandemic events. It is more than a little ironic that I write this chapter in the middle of the most awe inspiring and awful healthcare crisis to occur in the modern world, the COVID-19 pandemic. Many have compared this pandemic to the Spanish Flu of 1918, which may have caused as many as 50,000,000 deaths around the world. The Coronavirus has had its own devastating effects globally, while scientists across the globe rushed to find a vaccine, we still do not know what the coming months hold for our country or for the world.

The Need for Immediate Improvement

This virus is extremely contagious and indifferent to manmade boundaries, and infection can be fatal. It is, thus far, most acutely affecting those with a history of tobacco use, the elderly, and those who have pre-existing conditions that make them medically vulnerable. Most of those who have died thus far have fallen into one of these categories. However, the virus is so contagious that responsible political leaders across the globe have all but shut down their countries and their economies in a desperate effort to contain its spread. International travel has come to a virtual standstill and likely will not recover for some time. The list of economic devastation has become a long one with an ongoing threat of a recurrence, a resurgence, and an unknown future.

I am not trying to address the political, commercial, or psychological aspects of this crisis here. My goal is to link this epic healthcare event to a vision of the healthcare industry that has a greater ability to respond effectively to whatever challenges are coming in the future from a healthcare delivery perspective. We have an acute inelasticity in our healthcare system that is both local and global in character. We can't produce enough caregivers fast enough, nor can we replace them when they fall ill. We have too few hospital beds in some places and too many in others. We have similar inequities in the inventories of medical equipment and supplies. While we can and will have ways of solving the hospital room problem pretty quickly, as we did with mobile and field hospitals set up in the peak times of the virus, we cannot fix the caregiver problem quickly. We have witnessed this during weeks of caregivers volunteering to go into the hardest hit areas where the system had become overwhelmed by the volume of critically ill patients. The medical supply chain has become a national effort with manufacturing capacity being repurposed to make urgently needed Personal Protection Equipment as individuals felt even more vulnerable because they could not access masks, gloves, sanitizers, and other critical supplies. This has resulted in a psychological response that has reflected the physical and economic devastation brought by COVID-19.

I have learned so much over the last twenty years, but my learning has accelerated in the most recent six months. My curriculum included readings, conversations, observations, and realizations. I confess that things I thought not to be true are true, and things I thought were true are not. I can write all I want, but it will be no more valuable than a footstool if my efforts do not serve to catalyze changes in the way we think about healthcare in the United States. I am asking that you join me in this call to action. Bluntly, I need your help, and I offer you mine.

Improve Care at Every Level

So, let's start here with our medical personnel issues that recently became so visible to everyone but have been well known in the field for decades. First, we must address the issue of educating caregivers with a focus on nurses and medical doctors, without intending to offend any other caregiving profession by omission—a shout out to Doctors of Osteopathy, Chiropractic, and others!

The healthcare industry needs more LPNs and LVNs, and the profession should be more accessible to more people. We have an acute undersupply of nurses from communities of color and in communities of color. We need to accelerate their coursework so that they can be trained more quickly and move into the work-force more rapidly. This should be done as a one-year educational requirement for LPN/LVN licensing, a two-year educational requirement for RNs, with no test to be licensed as a nurse (of any stripe) if you have satisfied the educational requirement through an accredited nursing school, and a single test if you have graduated from an unaccredited domestic or foreign nursing school or medical school. Specialty nurses should be trained in four years, at the most, with the second two years focused exclusively on academic and clinical education directly related to the specialty.

We need to shed the unnecessary educational requirements that slow satisfaction of the prerequisites for licensing. Let us eliminate the excessive, duplicative series of state and federal tests required for licensing after all appropriate education at accredited institutions has been satisfied. Let's also look toward eliminating the excess of governmental and commercial regulations governing the delivery of healthcare services by qualified caregivers, many of which have created perverse incentives for everything from creative billing to insufficient treatment.

As our population ages and requires more caregivers to provide basic care and support, it will become more cost effective to rely upon LPNs/LVNs rather than RNs for certain aspects in the delivery of care. It has become clear that assisted care facilities, memory care facilities, and most hospitals are unable to function cost-effectively without these hardworking caregivers operating diligently on the front line of healthcare. These dedicated, trained professionals are ready and qualified to provide a broad range of important and necessary, but basic duties. They do not and should not require a four-year degree as a condition precedent to licensure. It is not that we are in such short supply for these nurses, but rather medical elitists in positions to hire new nurses still believe consistently that more education is better and thus hire professionals with a superset of education with little regard for the value of experience.

I have to offer an anecdote. My mother was living in an assisted care facility when she contracted pneumonia. Since the massive injuries she'd suffered in the plane crash that defined her health for a lifetime following her accident, she contracted pneumonia on average twice a year for most of the thirty-seven years she lived after the crash. As her primary caregiver, the hospital called me on December 29, 2010, to tell me that she was ready for discharge and could be moved from the hospital back to her assisted care facility. *Terrific!* I thought. Minutes later I got a call from the same discharge nurse who told me that my mother could not go to the assisted care facility. Instead, she had to go to a "rehab" facility. I didn't understand. "Why, and for how long?" I asked. "She needs to gain more strength and become ambulatory. It will probably take about thirty days," I was told.

"My mother has not been ambulatory for over ten years, and certainly won't become more ambulatory in thirty days, . . . what is the cost for this?" I asked.

The reply was one of the more stunning I have heard, "It is free. Why do you care?"

After considerable wrangling and winnowing down the time to only three to five days with the discharge nurse, I met my mother at the rehab facility where she was to be housed in a semi-private room with no television, telephone, or radio. Furious but still conversational, I asked the nurse at the rehab facility how long my mother would be there. The right answer would have been, "She can be discharged now." A less right but still tenable answer would have been "In three to five days" as the discharge nurse had communicated. Instead, the answer was "probably thirty days." I demanded that the rehab nurse review my mother's recent medical history and her trauma history only to have the visibly frustrated rehab nurse leave in a huff. I discharged my mother and returned her to the assisted care facility three days later.

The real reason my mother had to go to the rehab facility was that the assisted care facility *refused* to let her return to their care. They did not employ enough LPNs to care for those living at the assisted care facility, and they did not want to pay existing staff time and a half for overtime work. I can only empathize with any reader who experiences similar conundrums when faced with family or self-care!

I offer this anecdote to illustrate the point that we need more nurses, and that this will be even more critical as our people age. We also need to encourage future caregivers properly. The reality is likely different at each school, but the degree conferred by most nursing schools is either an ADN or a BSN, which qualifies you to take the NCLEX-PN exam. Let's not encourage students to suffer the expense and lost opportunity cost of an additional full year of study in order to complete five classes. Admittedly, those registered nurses seeking to practice in medical specialties may require additional education pertinent to their specialty, but that is a somewhat different point. Pro-nursing literature consistently advocates for additional education, encouraging students to get a masters or a PhD in nursing, though it is very hard to make economic sense of, find a medical justification for, or describe the practical need for the advanced degree. The need for a steady supply of nurses bumps up against the bias of the education industry advocating for the greater time in school, with educators happy to cite studies with poor methodologies boasting better medical care coming from BSNs than ADNs. To the contrary, "Although several studies have been undertaken, no definite conclusion has been reached about the relationship between nurse staffing [degrees] in hospitals and patient outcomes. Limitations of many of these studies include small sample size and the use of inconsistent measures of staffing levels."[1] Providing the right guidance as to what educational requirements are needed is crucial to the reform needed.

Experience and Competency in Nursing

Still more of an issue is the failure to consider experience levels when evaluating nurse competencies. Does any study really suggest that a first year BSN is more valuable (expressed as compensation) or likely to deliver a higher quality of care (expressed as mortality rate or complication rate) than a three-, five-, or ten-year LPN? Though these are complicated issues that are difficult to measure without the so beloved empirical support demanded by the medical profession itself, the question needs to be asked if we are to match our supply of nursing professionals to our need.

The ugly truth here is that nursing may be more properly considered to be a trade. Being a trade rather than a profession is no less noble, but the distinction allows us to think about educational requirements differently. More directly, considering nursing to be a trade rather than a profession provides a proper justification to streamline the educational requirements while allowing a delineation for moving from nursing to skilled or specialty nursing, which may be a profession due to the necessary additional educational requirements of specialized care coupled with the additional responsibility and autonomy nursing specialists have.

To sum, there is a lot of room to streamline the educational prerequisites for nursing, just as there are many reasons to eliminate the licensing exams for physicians if the student has graduated from a program at an accredited school. We should take advantage of the improvements in education that have occurred since Flexner wrote his report in 1910. That we have not done so is an indictment of far more than students, it is an indictment of all schools, colleges, universities, and educators!

Certainly, we have made great strides in primary, secondary, undergraduate, and graduate schools. We must also take advantage of technological advances that make the education more accessible through advance in distance learning.

Technology has not only shaped how we learn and what we learn, it also helps us with what we do not need to learn. Gamification, online classes, and online research have all affected how we learn. For good or for bad, the web, state and federal agencies, and local school districts have guided us with what we learn, meaning the content we ingest and, hopefully, synthesize. Just as importantly, technology has shown us what we do not need to learn. Just as the calculator may have started an unintended revolution over fifty years ago, Excel and other tools and their progeny have accelerated our ability to "go up a level" and focus on how to solve problems on a much broader scale while spending less time on basic functions.

But streamlining the educational prerequisites is only part of the answer. The adoption and integration of streamlined education, technology, and a culture that is led by those who embrace these changes can lead to the cascading of increasing degrees of responsibility. Where once only a doctor might be able to administer a particular invasive test or screening, over time that task can be relegated to others in the professional hierarchy. Registered nurses can do the job for which they have been educated and trained by moving regulators and medical elitists aside. Nurses should be, just as doctors should be, permitted in every jurisdiction to develop care plans, monitor patients in clinical environments and out of clinical environments, prescribe medications, and take on other responsibilities currently reserved only for physicians.

Another of my favorite of all quotes from my research is: "If the states were allowed to dictate the standards for testing, the requirements would be all over the map."

During the Coronavirus pandemic, the president issued an executive order authorizing the cross-border practice of medicine, including the ability to practice across state lines and the use of telemedicine. While this order was issued in the middle of a crisis, we might ask why it cannot stand once the crisis has ended. However, even the reporting shows the issues succinctly. Noting the concerns of regulators and providers, CNN reported "Telemedicine's growth has been hampered by multiple layers of federal and state regulation, which limited it largely to underserved areas or boutique providers. Also, many doctors have been hesitant to treat online, in part because of questions of how they'll get paid."[2]

Consider though that the lack of access to affordable, healthy food choices or affordable, quality medical services are matters not determined by state lines, but rather by other, unseen borders born out of historical, often commercial, interests that range from zoning to demographics. A caregiver familiar with the community in which their patient lives will be better positioned to advise the patient because that caregiver will appreciate the context and understand the other factors contributing to the patient's health conditions.

Telemedicine can also be helpful when the patient is too far from the caregiver and the particular issue is identifiable and discreet enough that it can be resolved without a physical examination. For example, I had a painful rash. I called my GP who had me take photos and email the photos to him using my smartphone. With the images at hand, he was able to ask a me couple of question and correctly diagnose the problem as shingles and he called in a prescription. I picked the medication up, and shortly thereafter my problem was resolved. The future of healthcare must be grounded in longitudinal relationships and delivered through the best available supporting technology.

Healthcare Needs to Include a Focus on Health

The future of healthcare must include a focus on health. This sounds so obvious but has strangely not been the model . . . ever.

The model should be reward people for keeping patients well, not create incentives to cure preventable illness. Consider what would happen if this occurred, and we did not need to build hospitals for years to come because the current facilities were more than adequate to accommodate the increase in population.

The CDC reported that the United States had 2,813,503 deaths in 2017. If we'd been able to eliminate heart disease and cancer, the number would have been reduced by about 650,000.[3] In addition, effective preventative care could have also reduced costs associated with treating heart disease by about $220 billion annually according to the CDC.

We are starting to see variations of this in the form of "population health management." This concept can be substantially advanced. I would like to see payments made to primary care practitioners much like or, ideally, included in (or bundled with) gym memberships, rec center memberships, or other health or fitness club memberships. These payments should also be applied to the deductible obligation for insurance. This would economically liberate individuals to go to their physicians more frequently, and more frequent visits would encourage the development of human relationships with caregivers, which would provide the contextual and longitudinal understanding of the patient and their healthcare needs and resources.

Population health management will not drive governmental regulation changes, but it has already impacted some commercial regulation changes. Insurance companies have for some time been experimenting with different payment models. One example is a payment per patient per month for routine care by the insurance company to the caregiver. The caregivers love this model because it provides greater certainty around cash flow and revenue. The future model should really be one where the payment is by the patient directly to the caregiver The morass of state and federal regulations creates a maze through which the physician must navigate in order to seek payment, and this can be mitigated in large part for those participating in this kind of program. Caregivers would then also be free to use the kinds of technology they've found most useful and cost-effective without worrying about reimbursement from an insurance company. Telemedicine should be at the forefront of these technologies, and it should be paid for by insurance companies or, better yet, by patients included in the membership fee model described above. Just as people are able to buy other goods and services through their smartphones, immediate, direct payment by the patient to the practitioner for telemedicine services could be facilitated through phone payments.

While some conditions warrant a visit to the doctor's office, most physician visits are scheduled in six-minute increments. It may take longer to get from the parking lot to the doctor's office than it does for the doctor to see the patient. Consider the additional aggravation of getting to the office (a profound hardship for many in blighted communities, rural communities, and for the elderly, the disabled, and others). The return trip is no better. Expanding patient access and the system's capacity to support telemedicine should be made a priority.

Currently, we have broadband deserts in urban areas and rural areas, but this does not need to be so. Let's cross the aisle and make it a bi-partisan initiative to make broadband available throughout the country and provide something like a video conferencing capability so that doctors can "see" their patients from their home or office without either party driving to see the other. Not only does the expansion of broadband access serve the health and economic interest for all stakeholders in the healthcare system, the expense does not have to be that great if we leverage rights of way and easements owned by the town, county, state, or federal government.

In looking to a future fully supported by the technologies we rely on to organize our lives at almost every level, beyond videoconferencing, we might look to software providers who should make healthcare technology interoperable and seamless, able to collect, store, and share all healthcare data for each individual. Failure to do so reflects a commercial interest and not a privacy concern or a technology concern. The data ingested by the patient's medical applications should be owned by the patient who can allow physicians and labs to do only those things to which the patient consents, and that consent is granted by the patient through a simple, easy to read document the acceptance of which is not a precondition to using the technology itself.

This patient data could be stored "in the cloud" where it would be periodically—as determined by the needs or desires of the patient and their primary care provider—synced with a cognitive computing capability, which would be a part of a health plan developed in conjunction with the primary care physician that would evaluate the sum of the healthcare data, identify trends of concern, and make recommendations for appropriate tests or doctors' visits, as needed.

The electronic healthcare record in the cloud would also allow for smart devices to input information from heart rate monitors, EKGs, diabetes and other blood tests, eye exams, and other self-administered tests along with any symptoms causing particular concerns about health or illness. The cognitive computing capability will make recommendations on care plans, medications, or physician visits that would be reviewed and approved by the caregiver. The technology could even be sufficiently integrated to schedule the visit with the doctor via videoconference. If an in-person visit is required, the technology can also arrange a ride with Uber or Lyft.

These AI-generated observations and recommendations would be monitored by nurses who will bring aberrations and abnormalities to the attention of a physician, where appropriate. All this technology exists right now! There is no reason, in fact no excuse, for it not being ubiquitous in access and use.

Doctors are critical to our system in a different way. They have been assigned the role of the brains of the healthcare system. Far too often, doctors, especially surgeons, take that too literally. There is a long-running joke in healthcare: "What is the difference between God and a surgeon? God doesn't think he is a surgeon."

One would think that if the doctor is so smart, he or she will ask a question and listen to the answer. A good friend, one of the most respected cardiologists in Dallas, told me that the average time it takes before a doctor will interrupt a patient is ten seconds. His point was "If you don't interrupt the patient, they might tell you what is wrong."

In many ways, this is unsurprising. It is quite understandable that doctors would grow impatient over time, seeing far too many patients who either fail or refuse to take appropriate actions for their own health, taking steps to educate themselves. Over time, doctors can get frustrated with the environment. At the same time, some doctors have the propensity to be the worst of the trophy generation. Raised from inception to be the smartest in their class, the highest achiever in every endeavor, they pursue recognition and fortify that with grades that support the praise.

It is expected that college students who become medical students who become doctors will have learned a lot! Measured in quantifiable academic terms, like grade point averages, doctors are necessarily smart, but it is possible that they have not learned the right things. Ethics, accounting, and leadership are all important topics in which students must invest themselves. It is important, after all, to know right from wrong, how businesses work, and how to lead teams. These are not topics either taken or taken seriously as prerequisites to medical licensure.

Lest you think I am eager to expand the educational requirements for doctors, let me quickly make it clear that is not the case. Just like my dream for nurses, the education of doctors should be streamlined in terms of the time required and altered in content. The replacement content should move unnecessary electives out and relevant subjects into their spots.

With the points on education and licensure already discussed, we can now imagine a greater supply of doctors and a greater supply of different kinds of doctors. The cost of becoming a doctor should drop precipitously if we were to make the training to become a doctor equal in educational length to that needed to become a lawyer or to earn some other form of doctoral degree. But the vision needs to go beyond that to include the creation of additional medical, dental, and other educational institutions that educate caregivers in the healthcare professions and to expand access to those professions.

Reducing the cost of becoming a doctor would allow more students who desire to become doctors to do so. We should focus the core educational requirements for all healthcare professionals on making the jobs more accessible to more people. We need to engage different types of people and to employ different types of thinking to solve the problems of the human race. The marketplace of ideas will sift through bad ideas and bad people, if need be, to get the right answers adopted.

Reducing the cost of becoming a healthcare professional and creating a greater supply of those professionals are important foundational elements for the future of healthcare. We can do more. The physician should be the "prime contractor" for the services he or she renders to any patient, and the physician can direct the patient to get a lab test or a diagnostic image from a third party, just like a mechanic can tell someone to buy their own parts and the mechanic will install them. Similarly, the hospital should be the prime contractor for all services rendered in a surgery, assuming all responsibility for providing supplies, anesthesia, labor, and the overhead costs associated with conducting the surgery.

The idea of a single point of contact should also include standardized accounting principles and practices that are standardized. Similarly, insurance companies should be transparent with everything from the composition of their networks to their billing practices to the prices they obtain from care providers to the collection practices they employ. Patients, as consumers who spend money earned from hard work and good intentions, should be able to hold care providers and insurance companies, alike, accountable. This future state should also allow for a timely, cost-effective, easy to understand and follow process to request an accounting, understand the charges, and to lodge and resolve complaints.

With a single point of contact for billing, expanded HSAs, transparent pricing, and direct membership payment models with primary care providers, we should be able to change the nature of our relationship with insurance companies to one with better understanding, less risk, and lower costs for both parties. Each of these elements helps us know what our expenses and our direct financial responsibility related to healthcare will be. In addition, by improving the frequency of the patient's interactions with the primary care provider and improving the technology associated with care by capturing more data and better data coupled with artificial intelligence, we should have fewer unanticipated healthcare problems or expenses. With a more proactive care model, anticipated expenses can be budgeted and paid for with greater clarity.

With the healthcare market reflecting consumer pressures and demands, prices will decrease, and quality will increase. These improvements for the 60% will beneficially impact the future of Medicaid by having access to good care at prices fair to the physician and fair to Medicaid, not a percentage of cost (cost, not price). Further, aid from state and federal governments through Medicaid and other medical programs like it should not be cut off abruptly but feathered down from 100% to 0% coverage so that we allow promotions and corresponding raises that encourage vocational and professional development by healthcare professionals. I have a dream that the "feathering" will take the form of contributions into an HSA being matched on a multiple to one basis, thus, again, encouraging personal responsibility, vocational and professional development, and the corresponding mobility between the classes. We will always have people in need, and, hopefully, we will always have people who graduate from one degree of need to a lesser degree of need. The Solution contemplates that improvement in circumstances will be enhanced by focusing on changing the healthcare consumer's economic circumstances over time.

Adoption of these proposals should extend life—an implicit goal—while enhancing the quality of life. Life expectancy for males is now approximately seventy-eight years, and it is eighty-three years for females. If we can make progress on heart disease, COPD, and obesity, life expectancy and quality of life will increase substantially. This should lead, culturally and commercially, to the elimination of mandatory retirements, particularly elimination of mandatory retirements at age sixty-two or sixty-five as required by many firms today.

Admittedly, I am of the opinion that retiring from work altogether is a bad idea, perhaps because I love my work or perhaps because my father-in-law is eighty-six and still working or perhaps because House Speaker Nancy Pelosi is eighty years old, former Secretary of State Madeline Albright is eighty-three, George Shultz and Henry Kissinger are both in their nineties, and all of these leaders are still doing important work. At some point, we will all perish at which time you should be able to leave proceeds of your HSA to your spouse, to your children, or to whomever else you would like to designate—as you would any other asset you have built and protected—creating a better psychological, physical, and financial future.

It would be wonderful to embrace a future where a greater percentage of patients engage in human relationships with their primary care physicians and work with them to develop health plans and prepare themselves for a long life of healthy living. With improved technology, streamlined administration, and innovative membership payment models, primary care physicians may just have enough time to not only keep current with current medical literature but also with advances in our understanding of nutrition, exercise, faith, and meditation. The health plan would include comprehensive plans for exercise, improved daily habits, sleep, nutrition, and appropriate therapies, and it would be developed with inputs from the patient, and existing technology would be made available and collaborative by inviting nurses in the primary care physician's office to monitor progress.

With the model established and the goals fixed on the horizon, we can then dream that governments, corporations, and representatives from the healthcare profession will come together as stakeholders to consider the broader issues of health exogenous to the control or behavior of the individual. This is their calling, their province, their opportunity, and the obligation for which they were each uniquely built. The cooperation of governments requires more thoughtful consideration of zoning issues such as placement of light and heavy industry, location of landfills, access to clean water and healthy food, access to parks, and access to good transportation networks. Contemporary literature calls these, collectively and in addition to other factors, the social determinants of health. Recognizing that the future cannot be perfect, I dream of leaders coming together to think through these issues and take the health of the population they serve into consideration when making decisions that may adversely impact some or all of these factors to the detriment of the community's health.

Finally, I dream of a compassionate, consumer-driven healthcare system that serves the entirety of our nation as equally as is possible. We must expand access to healthcare by increasing the physical presence of healthcare resources in underserved areas and use technology where it is economically impossible to justify having services or where there are too few people to support the business. We must universally embrace the notion that no child, no adult, and no family should be reluctant to go to a doctor or nurse because of the color of their skin or because the price is out of reach or because they fear the unknown. The future must also include compassion to be delivered just as evenly and equally as the services themselves, and compassion must have a role in treatment decisions that equals or exceeds the quality of the empirical research supporting the recommended course of action that the caregiver delivers to their patient.

Conclusion
THE STORY ENDS
WITH RESOLVE

The pandemic we are now in and, by the time this book is published, hopefully the world will be well through, has provided an opportunity to revisit the design of the US healthcare delivery and payment system. The 60% Solution offers a way to do that based on existing tools and a familiar paradigm. It will work. As is the case with other highly regulated industries, healthcare needs to go through periodic transformation that is not evolutionary in nature. That "rethink" is best served by a return to focus on values that are shared throughout the industry and from which all regulations are derived. We may or may not be at the point where we have the social and political will to undertake that transformation, but the recent pandemic has certainly provided the kind of upheaval that calls out for fresh thinking. The 60% Solution will do much good by embracing some underlying shared values. Rules, regulations, operating procedures and protocols, and the culture of caregiving organizations should be reasonably derived from a set of values shared by all stakeholders in the industry.

I once was thrust into an unexpected parenting moment. It was unexpected because, under directive, I had been told to support whatever my wife said in the form of disciplinary actions. On this occasion, I was called to the frontline and told "talk to him!" In what can only be described as a Solomonic intervention I said:

> Right now, from a developmental psychology perspective, you are trying to loosen the apron strings from your mother and gain more independence. Your mother and I are looking at your decisions and determining whether or not the judgment you are exercising merits that independence. So, what is judgment? I define judgment as the application of your values to the fact pattern before you to make a decision. You get your values from Scripture, the dining room table, friends you respect, and others. You learn how to apply those values through an apprenticeship. You watch how others apply values, like your mother and me. So, the judgment you exercised last night fell short. Do we need to spend time at the table discussing values or how to apply them?

I will say that the response I received was more animated and less eloquent than desired, but my remarks caused me to think about how the same dynamic works in industry. In fact, when you think about it, the same can be said for virtually any professional services firm. Where parents are mentors at home, leaders are mentors at work. Whether it is consulting, accounting, legal practice, or some other profession, the model is similar. The entry level employee might be an associate who becomes a senior associate who becomes an engagement director who becomes a junior partner who becomes a principal. The titles might be different, but the progression is largely similar.

The idea is that the firm is organically teaching its team, through introduction or reinforcement, what those values are and how to apply them. Rather than Scripture, though it may link to such, the firm is using the circumstance of the client or the circumstance of the team to show how to advise, manage, or lead. They are looking at the facts or circumstances before the team and determining how to apply the values of the firm to address the facts before the team to produce a values-based outcome.

Let me offer a final, personal example. I developed the early stages of my own professionalism at a company called EDS. Those to whom I looked up to taught me three essential things: "Take care of your team." "Get to know your team." "Know what motivates every member of your team." In other words, through their culture, I was taught what the group valued and that the group, itself, was valued.

I was given the opportunity to lead a team of 125 people to pursue a sales opportunity with a total contract value in excess of $4 billion. Not one person on the team worked for me, meaning that I did not have the authority to hire, fire, or discipline any of them. We worked seven days a week for four months, often out of town for two or more weeks at a time. I would, at my own expense, bring full coolers of bottled water, soft drinks, fresh fruit, and snacks and I took the initiative to personally restock printers with paper and pick up the area in order to keep everyone focused on the task at hand and working for the greater goal that we were all working toward. I did this myself, usually at midnight or later on Saturday night so as not to interrupt anyone, and to keep the re-stocking and cleaning work anonymous.

Our work, if successful, would produce jobs and professional opportunities for thousands of people for the next ten years, at least. When our work produced a winning result, I wrote, by hand, 125 personal thank you notes. Every member of the team got one. Twenty-five years later, I am still friendly with many of those colleagues, and I continue to get Christmas cards from some of them. That spirit of "taking care of the team" that was instilled through the group was a shared value of all, if not when they began, certainly through consistent action by the team members.

When law firms, consulting firms, or accounting firms are started, the senior partners use broad terms to lay out their firm's values: "Always do what is in the best interest of the client"; "Always disclose conflicts"; "Avoid even the appearance of impropriety." Over time, however, mistakes are made. First-line managers then put in place rules that are then "codified" or written into something called a policy manual or an employee manual. The act of writing the rule down so that someone else won't make the same mistake is misguided, counterproductive, and encourages behavior that should not be encouraged. Instead of the individual doing what they thought was right, the individual now must (a) be aware of the rule, (b) be subject to penalty for not abiding by the rule, and (c) be encouraged to follow rules rather than guide their behavior and actions by what is right in a given situation.

This shift is game-changing for such companies, because the codification shifts the employees' responsibility from understanding the values to understanding the rules. Worse, the application of the rules changes the nature of the action from judgment to decision. "Decision" is merely the question of whether or not the answer is yes or no, meaning that the facts meet the pattern embedded in the rule or they do not. Either the rule applies, or it does not apply.

Moving from decisions based on the application of values to decisions based on rules is a pivotal point, because it removes judgment out of the hands of the employee, manager, supervisor, or whomever else is making the decision. The person has gone from an individual and independent thinker to a jobsworth, or one who applies rules at the expense of common sense. We have taken responsibility out of culture and replaced it with enforcement.

Professor Ichak Adizes has written extensively about this shift change in mindset. If the business is running by the rules, it may not be running in accordance with its own values. When things seem to be running smoothly, management may think they are doing their job, but innovation, customer service, and other vital attributes of their work may not be evolving to meet changing needs, and that is when problems are likely to appear. The corporate entity seems okay, but it is increasingly relying on precedent and can easily defer taking risk, using judgment, or assuming responsibility.

A jobsworth won't be fired for applying the rules, but markets change, value propositions change, and products and services change. The common traits that hold the culture of the company together are the values, as static rules start to increasingly miss the mark. Further, rules beget rules as the patchwork expands to address new problems created by the rules, and the organization's vital culture erodes. Thus, new rules and policies propagate at an increasing rate of speed. Dr. Adizes wrote: "The centers of power are gradually shifting. Corporate staff positions such as finance, accounting, HR, legal, and risk management are gaining power at the expense of marketing, sales and production. Intuition and judgment play decreasing roles as facts, figures, and detailed analyses begin to rule the day."[1]

Another example from my days at EDS helps to flesh this out. A customer in Phoenix, Arizona, called the EDS account manager in Dallas at his home on a Saturday. The customer's midrange computer was down, and it needed a part to be repaired. The account manager in Dallas called the inventory manager in Dallas. They met at the warehouse, the account manager picked up the part, went to the airport, purchased a plane ticket, and flew to Phoenix that same day. The part was installed, the computer repaired, the customer was happy, and remitted payment for the part and the extraordinary delivery expenses on Monday. Note that countless "rules" were violated by the account manager. There was no "trouble ticket" called in to an 800 number. There was no purchase order. There was no pre-payment. The EDS account manager did not seek or obtain "manager approval" to get the part from inventory or to travel to Phoenix. However, the customer's problem was resolved, which upheld the company's highest value, customer satisfaction. Had the rules been followed, hours, days, or weeks of computing time and customer productivity would have been lost and the customer relationship would have suffered. Because the account manager's focus was on the greater value of customer satisfaction, the customer remained a customer well into the future and the account manager was applauded by his manager.

Why do I raise this and what does it have to do with the example given from my home life or my prior work life? The concern was not that our adolescent broke a rule, but rather that our adolescent was not acting in a manner consistent with our family values. At the other end of the spectrum is the example where my mother was sent to rehab despite everyone in the process knowing that my mother would derive no medical benefit by in going to rehab, but there was a rule that the nurse could, if she wanted to, rely on in order to require my mother go to rehab. If the "value" was to do what was best for my mother, the better decision would be to send my mother to her home.

Instead, the "rule" provided cover for a decision which was not in my mother's best interest, which masked the real reason for not sending her home.

Our current approach to healthcare is a patchwork of values, and, increasingly, rules, adopted from different times, and we've not had taken the opportunity to reevaluate how they fit together or considered how we might modernize them to better fit ongoing growth and the changing demands our society has placed on our healthcare system since the days of Abraham Flexner and William Osler. Healthcare today confronts demands such as or produced by: the increased number of people needing eldercare or access to residential care facilities, limited access to primary care physicians, the advent of medical deserts, the unequal distribution of healthcare services, the increased ability to solve more problems with over-the-counter medication, and more tangibly, the need to change everything from door widths to seat strength to elevator motor strength to accommodate obese patients. Our healthcare system's ability to meet these changing demands has been compromised because we have long ago left behind values and our caregivers are ensnared in commercial regulation from insurance companies that provide all manner of rules for prescribing what course of treatment is acceptable to qualify for a contract, to keep a contract, or to get paid under a contract with the corresponding insurance company.

Added to commercial regulation is an increasingly complex web of federal regulations emanating from Congress, HUD, HHS, and other bureaucracies addressing everything from technology to privacy . . . and that is just at the federal level. Remember that the states are responsible for putting in place regulations related to the health and safety of their citizens, which produces another layer of governmental regulations to

be navigated as each state has its own version of federal departments, agencies, and corresponding rules to be enforced. The
same is true for cities, counties, and towns of a sufficient size
to have the scale needed to warrant their creation. Still more
vexing is that many hospitals are both functional parts of an
educational system and are organized in something called a
"hospital utility district" with its own set of rules. Now, you
have some idea of the multiplicity of layers of rules that have
driven us farther from the guiding principles and shared values
of the stakeholders in the healthcare system.

Then, you have the corporate rules of the system in which
the doctor, nurse, or other caregiver operates. These govern
the day-to-day activities of the caregivers for every conceivable
case the caregiver may encounter. One could assert that for any
given decision to be made about a particular patient's course
of care, there are five or more rules that dictate the action that
"should" be taken which are five to seven generations of regulations removed from the values those rules were intended to
codify.

When an Unstoppable Force Hits an Immobile Object, Loud Noise Occurs

A few years ago, I was advising the board of a hospital on a
large transaction they were considering. This hospital was over
fifty years old and was considered a safety net hospital for the
region. It billed over $3 billion every year. The hospitals' cre-
dentialed physicians were some of the best in their fields in the
United States, and some of them were the best in the world.
The hospital was enormously respected for the work that it did,
particularly in the areas of trauma and chronic illness.

The hospital's board was made up of physicians, local business
leaders unfamiliar with healthcare, and others. The management

team included a CEO who was a dearly beloved physician who still did rounds once a week and attend to his own patients. He was terrific at raising money for the hospital, because he was beloved and had been there for so long.

It would be fair to say that the CEO loathed change—if you consider the word *abhor* stronger than *loathe,* then he abhorred change. He could not or would not make a decision about virtually anything, and worse yet, he frequently did not know what input, data, or procedure was required to make the decision. I am not only talking about his ignorance of what facts were need but his incapacity to understand about what rules applied to the decision-making process. Often, he did not know if he had the authority to make the decision, if his subordinate could make the decision, or if the board must make the decision. Still worse, he did not know what might cause the question at hand to require resolution or from what level of person that decision might flow. Though something like an "authority level matrix" did not exist, such a tool would never have made it to the clipboard the CEO carried with him at all times.

The transaction at hand was one that had a total contract value of more than $100 million. Ultimately, the board had to retain counsel to determine what rules the hospital had to follow to make the decision as to whether or not they could enter into the contract, what process must be followed to determine the list of vendors who could compete for the contract, and how to select the successful bidder. I was part of the consulting team hired by the board to develop, codify, and manage the process that would lead to a successful bidder and a signed contract.

Keep in mind that this was an administrative matter, yet, in the context of a major healthcare provider, a decision either way might result in lawsuits, penalties, and civil or potentially criminal implications. This had been borne out by the hospital's experience in an unrelated matter, this same hospital paid a civil settlement, with no finding of guilt or wrongdoing, of $2 million related to "overbilling Medicare and Medicaid" to the federal government. The risks were very real.

Let that sink in for a minute. In order for a civil settlement with the federal government to occur, there would have had to have been an investigation by the Federal Bureau of Investigation (FBI) and the Department of Justice (DOJ). Still more amazing, that investigation would have consumed a significant number of man hour resources from the DOJ, the hospital executives, the hospital's administrative staff, the doctors, the hospital's in house counsel, and outside counsel for more than a year. Again, let that sink in . . .

A large county hospital was investigated by the FBI and DOJ for potential fraud! No individual was charged, and no individual was asserted to have made off with a bunch of money. The county hospital was the recipient of the allegedly ill-gotten funds. The county paid the civil settlement.

The point here is that failing to follow all the rules, all of the time, is not only impractical, but likely impossible, and could be criminal. This experience exerted an influence over every subsequent decision taken by the hospital's management team; and, this was a billing matter, and not a medical issue.

In another instance, we worked with a hospital operated by a very well-known university. The university thought it would be a good cost-saving measure and a good educational opportunity to allow the students from the computer sciences department to manage all the IT needs of the hospital. There are many reasons why this could have been a good idea in any other industry. Regrettably, this is the healthcare industry where we must regulate privacy to excess and ignorance of applicable law may lead to fines, the closing a facility, or worse.

The students performing the IT work for the hospital owned and operated by the university thought it would be helpful to all caregivers, patients, and students to place as many Wi-Fi hotspots around the hospital as possible to provide convenient access to the hospital's network, its applications, and its data. This would allow the hospital's staff to access what they needed while walking around the hospital corridors, the cafeteria, or the outdoor patio. As long as the boundaries of the Wi-Fi access included the place you were standing or sitting, you had access to everything the hospital had to offer from inception to current. That meant that every lab test, patient visit, or other hospital record ever digitized was accessible to anyone with a personal computer, smartphone, or tablet. It also meant the financial systems, payment information, and other sensitive information were also available.

Of course, security was not a concern to the students, so there was no password requirement set up to access the network, the applications, or the data. This was clearly a violation of HIPAA and, as soon as we learned of it, our greatest fear was that this hospital would be the first in the nation to be closed for HIPAA violations. Our report was submitted to the hospital's General Counsel under protection of attorney-client privilege. The point of the story is not that these well-intended but incautious IT students were not caught or punished, but rather that we may never know what information was taken inappropriately, used wrongly, or even altered to the detriment of a patient. So, there are instances where rules may be needed.

You may recall the earlier discussion of Professor Adizes and the lifecycle of a corporation where we drew the analogy to the movement away from the way that the company was run in the early days to what Dr. Adizes subsequently refers to as "The Fall" where there were so many rules and adherence to the rules had become the primary focus of leadership, that leadership was dominated by lawyers and accountants. The point of these true stories is that physicians, hospital administrators, and others have become more like those in control of companies of "The Fall," as Professor Adizes describes it. They share a compendium of rules some of which conflict with one another and some of which may be bad for the patient if applied in a rote fashion, and these rules come to take precedence over professional judgment about the best course of care for a patient.

As the power to make decisions shifts away from the values and focus of the organization, an unhealthy competition of interest begins to corrupt the decision-making process. These are not just stories of administrators, legislators, and bureaucrats. The administrators are increasingly at odds with the physicians over both administrative and clinical matters. Administrators must take actions that increase revenue and decrease cost in order to satisfy their stakeholders, whether they are a for-profit or not-for-profit entity. Physicians frequently see directives or constraints as inappropriate overreach on the part of administrators. As one physician friend told me, "I resigned all of my management and board positions because they did not want to hear what I told them. It was clear they were not interested."

To be fair, the administrators may say something similar in return: "Doctors just don't get it. We are subject to legal liability if we don't follow certain rules." Or "We have to run a business that makes money in order to treat patients with the degree of care sought by the complaining physician. Don't they understand that?"

The confluence of different educational backgrounds, behaviors, emotional states, stress levels, compensation, loyalties, economic interests, and other matters position the mission differently for each stakeholder. Instead of focusing on executing the mission of the practice or institution in a manner consistent with a set of shared values, we have confusion, competing agendas, risk, and degradation of care and trust.

Again, this brings us back to the example of my mother and the question of who was really directing her care when it was mandated that she must go to rehab after her bout of pneumonia. Who was really monitoring her intake of medicines, both to make certain that they were taken correctly and to make certain that they were not abused? What was done in pursuit of a mission? What values were exemplified in the actions taken by physicians or institutions? These are not rhetorical questions; they are questions to which I do not know the answer.

We Need a Course Correction

As we have seen a dramatic spike in hospital acquisitions of physician practices over recent years, we have seen that the doctors have become employees of the hospital system. Doctors are trained, highly knowledgeable professionals who were *never* trained or prepared to be employees, and some might assert that doctors are "unemployable" meaning that they have egos or convictions such that they will at all times resist taking direction from others.

Remember, doctors are taught that they hold human lives in their hands, and there are times when this is not metaphorical. Such responsibility must be anchored by values that permit the caregiver the flexibility to do what, in the requirements of that moment, needs to be done based on the sum of the training and experience of the physician. Subjecting that person to retribution or penalty for failing to obey rules issued by an administrator would seem to fly in the face of that responsibility and that judgment. At the same time, the rules to which the physician is subject were generated for a reason that made sense at the time of its origin.

Complicating matters further is the notion that the risk assumed by the healthcare provider is not matched to the reward. Because doctors are such a large expense, smaller systems with irregular cash flows have sought to use the payroll of physicians to support cash flow. Some smaller systems have gone to quarterly payments of the doctors only, while others have CFOs eager to trim the compensation packages of the doctors, as they are one of the largest expenses on the hospital's income statement. Either of these measures sends undesirable ripples through the system. Doctors and other caregivers subject to these actions become discontented, which manifests in the quality of care delivery.

There is also a financial consequence to devaluing and limiting the independence of doctors. Caregivers have student debt and other bills to pay, just like everyone else. If they accept a position with a system expecting to be paid an agreed amount on an agreed time interval, such as every two weeks, and then the system unilaterally changes that bargain, bad things happen to everyone who is a stakeholder in that healthcare ecosystem. I am not suggesting caregivers should be expected to be immune to economics. I am saying that incentives need to be changed and shaped to ensure delivery of excellent care and exemplary management with reasonable costs.

This is not an unusual tension. In fact, every business must create a balance between what might seem to be competing objectives. Examples of competing objectives faced by every business include things like customer satisfaction, price, cost, and employee satisfaction. Improvement of healthcare outcomes is an example of customer satisfaction, but managing expectations is also a contributing factor in customer satisfaction. We often hear of patients facing bad healthcare outcomes who praise their physicians for their compassion despite the outcome. At the same time, caregivers have increasing awareness of revenue opportunities but far less understanding of the cost implications and are almost gleeful in overworking nurses and others deemed or perceived by them as subordinates. The solution virtually every other business employs is to perform periodic evaluations and use objective metrics to evaluate the performance of all involved in providing patient care. The result is an increase in base pay or a bonus, which may be a fraction of or a multiple of their base pay. Healthcare should be no different.

We Need to Do More

Collectively, the commercial and governmental sagebrush of regulations demands a rethink. We must grab the lot of them and remake the entire model. I do not presume that we will start over altogether and specifically point out that The 60% Solution was built for political expedience. It does not require a new paradigm for anything, but instead builds on or does away with existing rules, regulations, and models. HSAs exist today. The technology for managing patient heath records and offering alternatives to in-person care exist today. Accounting rules exist today. Primary care physicians exist today.

I am reminded of the professional services model and the vignette offered at the beginning of this chapter on values leading to judgment. We can and should draw analogies from these practices to the practice of medicine. Certainly, there are differences between disparate business models, but there are also plenty of similarities.

In order to adopt and execute the things proposed throughout this book that make up The 60% Solution, the proposed changes need to be done in connection with some agreed principles based upon shared values and not just be another round of randomly placed, patched together regulations.

Returning to values is the way to begin that effort. While not intended to be a definitive list for any organization or for the industry, I support a short, practical list of dominant values like:

- Consumerism

- Relationships

- Compassion

- Customer Service

- Transparency

- Systems Thinking

- Personal accountability

- Safety

I caution the reader, even if the reader is an administrator, practice manager, physician, or nurse, not to simply take the bullet points above and adopt them as your own. For those of you familiar with the practice of writing corporate mission statements and corporate purpose statements, the process should be similar. These are starting points for thought and discussion. For those of you unfamiliar with that process, I encourage you to brace yourselves for an exhausting journey made worthwhile not by its conclusion but by recognizing that it is the beginning of a process of transformation that will be exciting, frustrating, contradictory, and illuminating all while being years or decades in the making.

Corporate America usually fails here. They write the mission statement and post it on the website they seldom, if ever, read. Where virtually all of corporate America fails in this exercise, and this caution is offered in an effort to prevent practitioners adopting this course of action from failing, is to link governance (meaning how do we make decisions), process, job responsibilities, compensation models, and other facets of the business. Instead, organizations need to link the mission statement to decisions and correlated activities. The best practices I have seen, again, start *every* meeting throughout the organization with a recitation of the corporate values. I have seen some require this be included in the meeting invitation such that the invitation cannot be sent if not included. Then make a point of stating what values are intended to be manifested in the application of these values to the decisions to be made at the meeting.

When it comes to human capital, link those values overtly to the criteria employed in hiring personnel. If the personnel do not hold the organization's values dear, they will not be a good fit over the near or long term. Link training plans, courses, evaluations, and compensation to objective criteria that are measured and reported on regularly. Set up HR and IT systems to make this process organic.

Adopt a similar approach to the process of selecting vendors and affiliate stakeholders. Take the time at different levels in the organization to share corporate values with the vendor or affiliate. Discuss the organization's values and inquire of the prospective vendor or affiliate whether they think this might impact the delivery of goods and services or the relationship between the entities. Look at their brand position, interview them, evaluate their corporate values in light of your own, then select them accordingly. Price is an important but seldom should it be the driving issue for tension and strife in these relationships. When there is conflict, shared values will make that conflict easier to tolerate and resolve.

Lastly, medicine and the technology around healthcare delivery is changing rapidly. That cascades into the delivery of healthcare as a business. That change will be constant. The good news is that having done the work suggested above will make that change easier, particularly if you connect the desired future state to the mission and values of the firm and then support each individual in the firm in creating their own link to their personal values. A failure to do this will enhance the probability of failure of the change management exercise.

It is my hope that the reader will leave this book with a vision of what needs to be done to change the healthcare system based on key values. There is no one set of values that I or anyone else can lay out for the industry—though I might like to do so. While I am arrogant enough to write this book, I am not arrogant enough to suggest that I alone serve as the Oracle of Delphi for the industry. No, those values should be developed through the hard, often unpleasant and universally undesired work of leaders and implemented with the steely discipline of a NASCAR pit crew.

This thinking about shared values should be introduced to caregivers at the beginning of their educational career. The values of the institutions they support should be discussed as contributing to the students' development and not for rote adoption. The reinforcement and evolution of values should occur consistently throughout the entirety of their academic and clinical education. Lastly, aspiring healthcare providers should embrace their residencies, internships, and fellowships with the mindset of an apprentice. Over time, the apprentice gets better at the practice of applying the values to improve the quality of life of their patients.

It is my hope that this extends beyond caregivers to everyone in the healthcare industry. Administrators, politicians, and bureaucrats alike should make certain that they are embracing the values stated above and applying them thoughtfully daily.

US caregivers are the envy of the world. Our researchers and research facilities are the envy of the world. Our healthcare professionals have courage, valor, and commitment and want to serve people, ease their pain, and make them well. In fact, while I have met many doctors who want to make a lot of money, I have never met one who offered that desire as the reason he or she went into the field of medicine.

Our healthcare industry can also be the envy of the world, but our regulatory and economic systems must be reframed to allow caregivers to realize their goals and ambitions. *Caregivers* is a term that has compassion embedded in it. We need to free that emotion resident in each caregiver from the constraints under which that compassion is currently placed, and let it blossom in the hearts and minds of every member of the industry.

ENDNOTES

Notes for the Introduction

1   See www.usatoday.com/story/tech/2018/06/22/cost-of-a-computer-the-year-you-were-born/36156373/. (Accessed January 4, 2021)

2   Copeland, Rob, Dana Mattioli and Melanie Evans. Ínside Google's Quest for Millions of Medical Records. The Wall Street Journal online. https://www.wsj.com/articles/paging-dr-google-how-the-tech-giant-is-laying-claim-to-health-data-11578719700#:~:text=In%20certain%20instances%2C%20the%20deals,people%20familiar%20with%20the%20deals. (Accessed January 10, 2021).

3   Merriam Webster online. https://www.merriam-webster.com/dictionary/compassion

4   The cite for the projected cost of Medicare is a post by John Daniel Davidson https://thefederalist.com/2015/07/31/medicare-medicaid-same-problems-50-years-ago/. (Accessed July 31, 2015)

5   Diamond, Dan. "10,000 People Are Now Enrolling In Medicare—Every Day." https://www.forbes.com/sites/dandiamond/2015/07/13/aging-in-america-10000-people-enrollin-medicare-every-day/?sh=634b7bf13657

Notes for Chapter 1

1   See www.dubberly.com/articles/stevejobs.html. Article published on 1 May 1 2012. (Accessed January 1, 2021)

2   Shrank, William H. MD, MSHS, Teresa L Rogstand MPH, Natasha Perkh MD MS. "Waste in the US Health Care System: Estimated Costs and Potential for Savings." JAMA Network. https://jamanetwork.com/journals/jama/article-abstract/2752664?guestAccessKey=bf8f9802-be69-4224-a67f-42bf2c53e027&utm_source=For_The_Media&utm_medium=referral&utm_campaign=ftm_links&utm_content=tfl&utm_term=100719 (Accessed January 10, 2021).

3   Tozzi, John. (Sept. 25, 2019). "Health Insurance Costs Surpass $20,000 Per Year, Hitting a Record." https://www.bloomberg.com/news/articles/2019-09-25/why-is-health-insurance-so-expensive-20-000-a-year-for-coverage (Accessed January 11, 2021).

4   primarycare Progress. "The Case for Primary Care." https://www.primarycareprogress.org/primary-care-case/#:~:text=People%20who%20have%20a%20primary,other%20outpatient%20care%20(6)

5   Khan FH, Hanif R, Tabassum R, Qidwai W, Nanji K. Patient Attitudes towards Physician Nonverbal Behaviors during Consultancy: Result from a Developing Country. *ISRN Family Med.* 2014;2014:473654. Published 2014 Feb 4. doi:10.1155/2014/473654

6   Health Information & the Law. "Who Owns Medical Records: 50 State Comparison." http://www.healthinfolaw.org/comparative-analysis/who-owns-medical-records-50-state-comparison. (Accessed January 10, 2021).

Notes for Chapter 2

1   See www.crnusa.org/resources/economic-impact-dietary-supplement-industry. See also nutrition.guerrillaeconomics.net/assets/site/res/CRN%20Methodology.pdf for "2016 Economic Impact of the Dietary Supplement Industry" published by John Dunham & Associates 32 Court St., Suite 207 Brooklyn, New York 11201.

2   See www.ncbi.nlm.nih.gov/pmc/articles/PMC2430660/. (Accessed January 4, 2021) See also "Status of nutrition education

in medical schools" by Kelly M Adams, Karen C Lindell, Martin Kohlmeier, Steven H Zeisel. *The American Journal of Clinical Nutrition*, Volume 83, Issue 4, April 2006, Pages 941S–944S, doi. org/10.1093/ajcn/83.4 941S. (Accessed June 1, 2009)

3   See www.aamc.org/system/files/c/2/451374-nutriritoneducationi nusmedschools.pdf. (Accessed January 4, 2021)

4   See Rosen RC, Rosekind M, Rosevear C, Cole WE, Dement WC. "Physician education in sleep and sleep disorders: a national survey of U.S. medical schools." *Sleep.* 1993 Apr;16(3):249-54. doi: 10.1093/sleep/16.3.249. PMID: 8506458.

5   See www.cdc.gov/physicalactivity/walking. (Accessed January 4, 2021)

6   See

7   See lcme.org/publications/. (Accessed January 4, 2021)

8   See scopeblog.stanford.edu/2015/01/27/why-establishing-a-health-baseline-is-a-critical-starting-point-for-achieving-future-health-goals/. (Accessed January 4, 2021)

9   See www.jhsph.edu/research/centers-and-institutes/johns-hopkins-primary-care-policy-center/definitions.html. (Accessed January 4, 2021)

10 See www.aafp.org/about/policies/all/family-medicine-roledefinition.html. (Accessed January 4, 2021)

11 Donaldson MS, Yordy KD, Lohr KN, et al., editors. Washington, DC: National Academies Press, 1996.

12 See www.ncbi.nlm.nih.gov/books/NBK232631/ (Accessed January 4, 2021) or Institute of Medicine (US) Committee on the Future of Primary Care; Donaldson MS, Yordy KD, Lohr KN, et al., editors. Washington, DC: National Academies Press (US); 1996.

13 See assets.americashealthrankings.org/app/uploads/ahrannual-2018.pdf, p. 23.

14 See healthblog.uofmhealth.org/childrens-health/when-and-why-a-teen-should-start-seeing-a-gynecologist. Courtenay Edelhart, March 4, 2020. (Accessed January 4, 2021)

15 See www.washingtonpost.com/health/america-to-face-a-shortage-of-primary-care-physicians-within-a-decade-or-so/2019/07/12/0cf144d0-a27d-11e9-bd56-eac6bb02d01d_story. html by Victoria Knight, July 15, 2019. (Accessed January 4, 2021)

16 See de.reuters.com/article/instant-article/idUSKBN1YK1Z4 by Linda Carrol. (Accessed on 1.4.21) citing Characteristics of Americans With Primary Care and Changes Over Time, 2002–2015 by David M. Levine, MD, MPH, MA[1,2]; Jeffrey A. Linder, MD, MPH[3]; Bruce E. Landon, MD, MBA, MSc[2,4,5].

17 For blacks' reluctance to get invasive screenings, see www.washingtonpost.com/outlook/2020/12/15/years-medical-abuse-make-black-americans-less-likely-trust-covid-vaccine/ by Dan Royles on December 15, 2020. (Accessed January 4, 2021)

18 Klea D. Bertakis, MD, MPH, Rahman Azari, PhD, Jay L. Helms, PhD, Edward J. Callahan, PhD, and John A. Robbins, MD, MHS published in the *J Fam Pract*. 2000 February; 49(2):147–152. See also www.mdedge.com/familymedicine/article/60747/womens-health/gender-differences-utilization-health-care-services/page/0/1.

19 See pubmed.ncbi.nlm.nih.gov/8917147/ or Norcross WA, Ramirez C, Palinkas LA. "The influence of women on the health care-seeking behavior of men." *J Fam Pract*. 1996 Nov;43(5):475–80. PMID: 8917147.

20 See www.religioustolerance.org/medical2.htm. (Accessed January 4, 2021)

21 See www.ncbi.nlm.nih.gov/pubmed/15333285 (Accessed January 4, 2021) or Boulis, AK, Long, JA. "Gender differences in the practice of adult primary care physicians." *J Womens Health* (Larchmt). 2004 Jul–Aug;13(6):703–12. doi: 10.1089/jwh.2004.13.703. PMID: 15333285.

22 See www.primarycareprogress.org/primary-care-case/. (Accessed January 4, 2021).

23 See www.oregon.gov/oha/hpa/dsi-pcpch/Pages/index.aspx. (Accessed January 4, 2021)

Notes for Chapter 3

1 See www2.census.gov/library/publications/1949/compendia/hist_stats_1789-1945/hist_stats_1789-1945-chD.pdf. (Accessed on 1.4.21)

2 Modern Healthcare. "Feds amassed $2.6 billion from 2019 healthcare fraud cases." https://www.modernhealthcare.com/legal/feds-amassed-26-billion-2019-healthcare-fraud-cases#:~:text=The%20department's%20recoveries%20from%20healthcare,and%20%242.1%20billion%20in%202017.

3   See www.kff.org/wp-content/uploads/2013/01/8122.pdf.
    (Accessed January 4, 2021)
4   Tax Policy Center. "Key Elements of the U.S. Tax System.
    https://www.taxpolicycenter.org/briefing-book/how-does-tax-
    exclusion-employer-sponsored-health-insurance-work (Accessed
    January 10, 2021).

Notes for Chapter 4

1   See www.careeraddict.com/top-10-most-boring-jobs-2015 by
    Ken Harrison on 4 November 2016. (Accessed January 4, 2021)
2   See truecostofhealthcare.org/hospital_financial_analysis/.
    (Accessed January 4, 2021)
3   See truecostofhealthcare.org/hospital_financial_analysis/.
    (Accessed January 4, 2021)
4   See hipaa.bsd.uchicago.edu/background.html.
    (Accessed on 1.4.21)
5   See #HL7WGM #healthIT #interoperability #HL7FHIR.
    (Accessed January 5, 2021).

Notes for Chapter 5

1   See www.usnews.com/news/best-countries/articles/2016-08-03/
    canadians-increasingly-come-to-us-for-health-care by Randi
    Druzin, Contributor, August 3, 2016.
2   Jason C. Pradarelli, MD, MS1; Mark A. Healy, MD, MS;
    Nicholas H. Osborne, MD, MS; Amir A. Ghaferi, MD,
    MS; Justin B. Dimick, MD, MPH; Hari Nathan, MD,
    PhD "Variation in Medicare Expenditures for Treating
    Perioperative Complications: The Cost of Rescue" JAMA Surg.
    2016;151(12):e163340. doi:10.1001/jamasurg.2016.3340 (Accessed
    December 21, 2016).
3   Rothbaum, Jonathan and Ashley Edwards. (9/10/19). "Survey
    Redesigns Make Comparison to Years Before 2017 Difficult."
    https://www.census.gov/library/stories/2019/09/us-median-
    household-income-not-significantly-different-from-2017.
    html#:~:text=U.S.%20Median%20Household%20Income%20
    Was,Not%20Significantly%20Different%20From%202017
    (Accessed January 12, 2021).

4   See www.usatoday.com/story/money/business/2018/06/06/
    health-care-costs-price-family-four/676046002/ by Guy
    Boulton, June 7, 2018.

5   See www.investopedia.com/articles/personal-finance/091015/
    why-high-earners-still-live-paychecktopaycheck.asp by Rebecca
    Lake, March 24, 2020.

6   See https://www.irs.gov/pub/irs-drop/rp-20-32.pdf

7   Miller, Stephen. (10/27/20). "2021 FSA contribution Cap
    Stays at $,750, Other Limits Tick Up. https://www.shrm.
    org/resourcesandtools/hr-topics/benefits/pages/2021-fsa-
    contribution-cap-and-other-colas.aspx#:~:text=While%20
    the%20IRS%202021%20pretax,employees%20to%20less%20
    than%20%242%2C750.&text=If%20employers%20provide%20
    health%20care,amount%20that%20employees%20can%20elect.
    (Accessed January 12, 2021).

8   See www.healthcare.gov/have-job-based-coverage/flexible-
    spending-accounts/. (Accessed on 1.5.21)

9   For a full list, see fsastore.com/FSA-Eligibility-List.aspx.
    (Accessed January 5, 2021).

10 See www.usatoday.com/story/money/business/2018/06/06/
    health-care-costs-price-family-four/676046002/ by Guy Boulton,
    June 7, 2018 and see www.wsj.com/articles/cost-of-employer-
    provided-health-coverage-passes-20-000-a-year-11569429000 by
    Anna Wilde Matthews on September 25, 2019.

11 See www.forbes.com/sites/zackfriedman/2019/01/11/live-
    paycheck-to-paycheck-government-shutdown/#7d90d5f94f10 by
    Zack Friedman on January 11, 2019; and CNBC says "4 out of 5."
    See also www.cnbc.com/2019/01/09/shutdown-highlights-that-
    4-in-5-us-workers-live-paycheck-to-paycheck.html by Emmie
    Martin on January 10, 2019.

Notes for Chapter 6

1   Bonner, Thomas Neville "Searching for Abraham Flexner."
    Academic Medicine. February 1998, 73 (2): 160–166.

2   "Abraham Flexner Papers—A Finding Aid to the Collection in the
    Library of Congress" (PDF). Library of Congress. *April 2010.* p. 4.

3   See Bonner above.

4   Abraham Flexner, *The American College*. New York: The Century Company, 1908, pp. 215–216.

5   See medlineplus.gov/ency/article/001936.htm. (Accessed January 5, 2021)

6   See www.brainyquote.com/authors/william-osler-quotes. (Accessed January 5, 2021)

7   See Osler's *"A Way of Life & Other Addresses, with Commentary and Annotations"* by Sir William Osler. 2001. Durham, NC: Duke University Press.

8   See daily.jstor.org/the-1910-report-that-unintentionally-disadvantaged-minority-doctors/ by Jessie Wright-Mendoza on May 3, 2019.

9   Mark E. Silverman, MD, T. Jock Murray, MD, and Charles S. Bryan, MD. *The Quotable Osler*. 2008. Philadelphia, PA: American College of Physicians, p. 91.

10 See www.amc.edu/BioethicsBlog/post.cfm/thoughts-on-flexner-and-professionalism-1915-and-2015 by Bruce White, DO, JD on September 8, 2015.

11 See www.cchpca.org/telehealth-policy/current-state-laws-and-reimbursement-policies?keyword=telehealth. (Accessed January 5, 2021)

12 Quotable Osler, p. 220.

13 See www.texmed.org/TexasMedicalLicense/. (Accessed January 5, 2021)

14 See www.tmb.state.tx.us/page/physician-applicants. (Accessed January 5, 2021)

15 See www.cms.gov/Medicare/Provider-Enrollment-and-Certification/MedicareProviderSupEnroll/downloads/EnrollmentSheet_WWWWH.pdf. (Accessed January 5, 2021)

16 Quotable Osler, p. 9.

17 See oig.hhs.gov/publications/docs/hcfac/FY2018-hcfac.pdf. (Accessed January 5, 2021)

18 See p. 10 oig.hhs.gov/publications/docs/hcfac/FY2018-hcfac.pdf. (Accessed January 5, 2021)

19 https://www.modernhealthcare.com/legal/feds-amassed-26-billion-2019-healthcare-fraud-cases#:~:text=The%20department's%20recoveries%20from%20healthcare,and%20%242.1%20billion%20in%202017

20 United States Department of Justice. (May 31, 2013). "Parkland Memorial Hospital Pays Nearly $1.4 Million to Resolve Allegations It Submitted Improper Physical Medicine and Rehabilitation Claims." https://www.justice.gov/usao-ndtx/pr/parkland-memorial-hospital-pays-nearly-14-million-resolve-allegations-it-submitted. (Accessed January 12, 2021).

21 See www.medicalbillingandcoding.org/learn-more-about-coding/. (Accessed on 1.5.21)

22 See www.nationmaster.com/country-info/stats/Health/Physicians/Per-1,000-people. (Accessed January 5, 2021)

23 See www.nationmaster.com/country-info/stats/Health/Hospital-beds/Per-1,000-people. (Accessed January 5, 2021)

24 See www.nationsencyclopedia.com/WorldStats/HNP-nurses.html. (Accessed January 5, 2021)

25 See www.usatoday.com/story/opinion/2018/07/31/high-maternal-death-rate-shames-america-developed-nations-editorials-debates/866752002/ by The Editorial Board, July 31, 2018.

26 Quotable Osler, p. 48.

27 See www.usa.gov/federal-agencies/food-and-drug-administration. (Accessed January 5, 2021)

28 See Evid. Based Med., 2017 Jun;22(3):88–92., doi: 10.1136/ebmed-2017-110704. Epub 2017 May 29.

29 See ebm.bmj.com/content/22/3/88 or Ebell MH, Sokol R, Lee A, et al, "How good is the evidence to support primary care practice?" *BMJ Evidence-Based Medicine* 2017; 22:88–92.

30 See www.ncbi.nlm.nih.gov/pmc/articles/PMC3599067/ or Ebben RH, Vloet LC, Verhofstad MH, Meijer S, Mintjes-de Groot JA, van Achterberg T. "Adherence to guidelines and protocols in the prehospital and emergency care setting: a systematic review." *Scand J Trauma Resusc Emerg* Med. 2013; 21:9. Published 2013 Feb 19. doi:10.1186/1757-7241-21-9

31 See "Compromised Compliance with Evidence-Based Guidelines" at www.researchgate.net/post/What_proportion_of_medicine_is_evidence-based by Constantine Konikidis on March 30, 2014.

32 See www.medicalbillingandcoding.org/learn-more-about-coding/. (Accessed January 5, 2021)

Notes for Chapter 7

1   See www.cna-aiic.ca/-/media/cna/page-content/pdf-en/
    rs_higher_levels_e.pdf?la=en&hash=7806DEEDED46A63A9
    4AA27545ED22999472F4019 or Needleman, J., Buerhaus, P.,
    Mattke, S., Stewart, M., Zelevinsky, K. (2002). "Nurse Staffing
    Levels and the quality of care in hospitals." *New England Journal of
    Medicine*, 346 (22), 1715–1722.

2   See www.cnn.com/2020/03/14/politics/telehealth-us-federal-
    response-coronavirus/index.html by Brian Fung and Tami Luby
    on March 14, 2020.

3   See www.cdc.gov/nchs/fastats/deaths.htm. (Accessed
    January 5, 2021)

Notes for the Conclusion

1   See adizes.com/lifecycle/lifecycle-the-fall/. (Accessed
    January 5, 2021)

ACKNOWLEDGMENTS

Where to begin? Acknowledgments commonly express an author's thanks for professional and emotional support, with one taking more prominence over the other based on the relationship the author has with the topic. My relationship with the topic of this book has been grounded in a family tragedy more dramatic than anything Shakespeare wrote. As a result of my personal connection to the issues and challenges surrounding my mother's lifelong need for healthcare after the tragic plane crash that changed all of our lives, I likely drew far more support than is normal from those whose unyielding commitment I so greatly appreciate.

I will start with the professional acknowledgments: Nancy Hancock has been a terrific professional and an integral part of this effort. Thankfully, she is as patient as she is loquacious. More thankfully, she can challenge, debate, argue, and conclude most often with an open mind. While subject to her personal and professional convictions, Nancy has been both persuasive and persuadable. This book would not be in print without her counsel and guidance.

Lori Martinsek and her team at Adept Content Solutions were not only tireless, but also relentlessly creative in turning out good recommendations and quick turns. Her good humor never waivered.

I am also indebted on many levels to my dear friends in Forum 2.0: Eric Affeldt, Jim Beckett, Jim Collet, Bob Delk, Tom Leppert, and Bruce Whitehead. They are all multi-faceted intellectuals and dear friends who have listened to my woes, given great counsel, and were early readers of the text. Eric went so far as to offer detailed feedback, and Jim Beckett helped me rethink the entire approach to publication. Thank you.

There are family members at the beginning of this story whose support has been uniformly positive, and generous for many decades. Mimi, or Mrs. James Julien Southerland Jr., my sister, Berkeley, or Mrs. Stephen McHugh, and "Uncle Jimmy," Capt. James Julien Southerland III, USN, Ret. have all been reliable, critical sources of strength and support in different ways.

Mimi was always the "iron fist in the velvet glove." Adept in the southern tradition of very elegant ladies, she was never one to raise her voice or use a coarse word or take a harsh tone. Yet, she was always a model of fierce loyalty and love. She'd been a single mother from the time her husband, a naval pilot, died in his *second* military plane crash during the Korean War, leaving her with three children age twelve and under. Always sweet, impeccably attired, and perfectly groomed, Mimi quietly told me that she never remarried because she could never love anyone as much as she'd loved her "Pug." Berkeley, Mom, and I lived with Mimi between my mother's marriages, and I learned all I know about love and strong values from her.

Berkeley has been the quiet rock for me since we were young, even before dealing with the tragedies, trials, and tribulations of our mother's accident and her years of need and care, all of which took place over decades. Despite being "quite a few years younger" than me, Berkeley is better read, more academically accomplished, and more orally demonstrative in her affection and disagreement. She has influenced students all over the world and provided unwavering loving support to her entire family. If I am to my family a fraction of what she is to hers, I will consider myself a success.

My "Uncle Jimmy" has also been there every step of the way. Despite his lifelong affliction with "Diehard Washington Redskin Fan Syndrome" (aka "Washington Football Club Fan Syndrome"), he has been a spiritual leader for me and for many others inside and outside of our family. His warm and soothing voice is always available at the other end of the telephone, and I cannot remember leaving a call without a smile on my face.

My mother is at the center of this story. She is the prologue, the catalyst, and the epilogue. If I know how to write at all, it is due to her. I started in the eighth grade by editing her essays and term papers when she went back to college to get her degree in English while being a wife and mother to four children and working part time for my father's law practice. While all sons love their mothers, my love for my mother is dwarfed by my respect for her. She was brave, indominable, tough, charming, and indefatigable.

While these family members were and remain fixed in my heart and mind, I genuinely struggle to find words that can convey my love for my wife. She has been consistently supportive, believing in me far more than I've believed in myself. I have said on many occasions that she has such depth that I have never found the bottom, and that I swim through her aesthetic. Wrapped in a breathtakingly beautiful exterior, her well-recognized beauty is her least significant quality. Her faith, conviction, values, and support are exemplary characteristics of the heart and soul of our family. She has challenged, encouraged, coaxed, and cajoled each of us, all with the noble intent of producing a desired outcome. She is gracious, gratitudinous, and always has a servant's heart.

My children have been a source of pride, comfort, love, and conviction. It's been said that you develop greatly as a person when you have children, and that is certainly the case with me. I have learned more than I could have imagined about compassion, empathy, and love from each of them. If they hurt, I hurt. If they suffer, I suffer. I am not unlike other parents, and that awareness makes this topic so important to me. Ashley, John, and Amanda have made me a better person, and, in many ways, this book has been written with the hope and optimism that their generation will benefit most from the adoption of some or all of the proposals offered in *The 60% Solution*.

ABOUT THE AUTHOR

T odd Furniss has over twenty-five years of global experience in private equity, consulting, and operations as a senior-level operating executive. He has implemented operations strategies that grew businesses in more than ten industries throughout the Americas, the European Union, and Asia. He currently serves as the CEO of gTC Group, a private firm dedicated to creating value for stakeholders in middle-market, technology-enabled business services, financial services, and healthcare companies and the correlated real estate. Todd has recently been appointed to serve as one of five board members of the North Central Texas Health Facilities Development Corporation that serves to facilitate the development of primary health care equipment and property to improve the general quality of care available to citizens in central Texas. His broad professional experience, coupled with life circumstances, has led him to passionately work to rectify our current healthcare system's shortcomings.

To learn more, see www.thesixtypercentsolution.com